FOR

LIFE

THE MEMOIRS OF A SISTERHOOD

By

A.ADDISON, C.JACKSON, L.MOORE, T.STRAITE

Tables of contents

A Vision/Introduction -- 6

Dedication--12

The Professional ---13

Poignant ---14

Perfection ---17

Proficient ---21

Promising Partnership--27

Privilege---43

Politics--49

Proponent--54

Peroration---61

Acknowledgments--71

Dedication---74

The Celebrity --75

The Journey to Forgiveness ------------------------------------77

   Grandmother--77

My Best Friend ---81

   The Final Blow --84

The Stages of Forgiveness --------------------------------------87

   Healing in Forgiveness ----------------------------------87

   Humiliation in Forgiveness------------------------------88

   Humiliation in Unforgiveness ---------------------------90

Guilt and Grief --- 91

Battling Self-Accountability with Forgiveness --------- 93

Learning Along the Road to Forgiveness ------------------ 95

Forgiveness Now vs. Forgiveness Then -------------------- 97

The End is Just the Beginning ----------------------------- 100

Acknowledgments --- 101

Dedication --- 106

The Unicorn --- 107

You Have a Purpose --- 108

My Journey to an Awakening ------------------------------ 109

Men. -- 109

Relationship Number One ------------------------------ 113

Relationship Number Two ------------------------------ 115

Relationship Number Three ---------------------------- 116

Relationship Number Four ------------------------------ 117

Rediscovery -- 122

Divine Connections --- 126

The Encounters --- 135

The Miracle of Healing ------------------------------------- 148

The Miracle of Life --- 155

Surprise Encounters --------------------------------------- 160

Acknowledgments --- 172

Dedication --- 176

The Preacher -- 178

The Call -- 182

Marriage and the Call; I Do and I Do ---------------------- 185

   Points to Ponder: --- 189

Finally Free: Totally Bound --------------------------------- 190

The Breaking Point -- 201

Preach Anyway -- 208

Why I Stayed -- 213

Fruit of the Spirit --- 220

ISLAND (In His Safety, Love and Newness Develop) --- 227

Released -- 229

Ministry after Divorce -------------------------------------- 234

Divine Connections -- 236

Faith Forward -- 239

Ownership -- 242

My New and Forever Husband is on the Horizon ------ 243

Acknowledgments-- 246

Closing -- 248

A Vision/Introduction

About two years ago, I, The Preacher, coined the phrase 4ever4life.

We, the Co-Authors, started to use it as a form of salutation/greeting to describe the bond between me and my girls.

Whenever we were together, just before departing we would always say that we loved each other, "4ever4life". We said it to each other, added it to the end of text messages, and even used it at the end of our social media posts. It seemed like more than a greeting or salutation, but I had no idea what else it was. I even remember suggesting to the girls that perhaps it was a tattoo that we were supposed to get and that we needed someone to design it for us.

It was on January 9th, 2020, that God revealed to me what 4ever4life really was. It was early afternoon, and I was on the brink of a nervous breakdown.

It was the first day of my layoff period from the job where we all became connected. All of the other members of the group had already been laid off except for one of us. After my departure, there was only one more of us left at this employer.

I worked a half-day and then left for home. I went to the mall just to walk around. I'd found myself with all of this new free time that I did not know what to do with. While I walked, I began feeling a little off. My breathing became labored--I was starting to have a panic attack. I now realize. My life was in a whirl spin already and the layoff just took it over the top.

I decided to leave the mall and head home because I was feeling really terrible. As I drove home, I started to feel progressively worse.

I called a girlfriend and told her what was happening to me just in case I did not make it home. She suggested that I go to the hospital since I was also experiencing chest pains. I declined. I just wanted to go home and lie down. I promised her that I would text to let her know that I made it home once I got there.

I remember pulling into the garage feeling really faint with my thoughts all over the place. In my head, there were so many things going on at once. I remember thinking this must be what a nervous breakdown feels like. I thought about us all being laid off, with families and responsibilities and no income.

As I walked up the stairs to my bedroom, I chanted the following scripture over and over. "Let this mind be in you, that is also in Christ Jesus" (Philippians 2:5 KJV). When I reached the top step just before turning into my room God said to me, "Forever for Life is a book. It's a collective effort that will be written by you and the girls. This is why you have been placed together." He even gave me the titles of each one's section.

I hurried to get into my room to write down what He had told me. After writing it down, I laid down to take a nap. When I woke up, I immediately called the girls and told them of my encounter with the Lord and the instructions that He had given. None of us questioned what had been asked of us. From the very beginning, each one of us was willing to be obedient.

Inside this book, broken down into four distinct sections, you are about to experience what an act of obedience looks like. We must admit that there have been hurdles and challenges along the way, but here it is. We have done what the Lord has asked us to do. We trust that due to our obedience, this book is already blessed, and we recognize that its ultimate purpose is to inspire you to greatness. Out of confusion and chaos, a masterpiece has been created.

Enjoy the ride that you are about to embark on. Be ready to embrace the newness that we will introduce you to. Be ready to be, forever for life, changed!

Note: All scripture quoted in New International Version (NIV) except where indicated.

Leslie

My two favorite people on earth call me Lez and Mum but you can call me Leslie.

I am an energetic, talkative wife to the best husband ever and mommy to the sweetest but sassiest little two-year-old. I was born and raised in Missouri City, Texas but I now reside in the suburbs of Raleigh, North Carolina. My most enjoyable pastimes are traveling, meeting new people, talking about different cultures, religions, and food. I also enjoy spending time with my family and friends who have become my family and dreaming inside million-dollar model homes.

Follow me on Social Media **eL.A.J.Moore**

Excerpt from book:
"Kindly speak your truth unapologetically through love, spend time getting to know your inner being, be your authentic self no matter what feathers you ruffle..."

<u>Dedication</u>

This section of this book is for my little beauty Arley Alexandria Moore, and all of her future girlfriends. You are loved, and I know you and your girlfriends will change the world!

The Professional

For as long as I can remember, I heard that I could be whatever I wanted to be in this world. As a little girl, I truly believed this statement, and no one could tell me otherwise because I knew how big my God was to me. I was the epitome of a strong-willed and ambitious girl; I stepped out on faith and made things happen even when it seemed like they couldn't. Throughout my life, my view of God changed several times. As I take you on my journey, we will dig deeper into the various seasons I've been through so that you can see how God perfectly orchestrated my life, even when it looked like complete trash with a capital T. Today, I see a lot of the same drive I had as a little girl pushing me to be the best version of myself. Nonetheless, I often wonder how the trajectory of my life would have changed had I not encountered some of the situations I called setbacks at the time, but in actuality, they were building me to be an even better *Professional*.

Poignant

What are you afraid of? What is it that's holding you back? Why haven't you pursued the thing or things you can't keep your mind off of? Who told you, you couldn't do it? When did your self-doubt start? Who caused your self-doubt?

It is a scientific fact that babies operate on a genius level because they are a blank slate without self-doubt holding them back. Their imagination isn't tainted with a glass ceiling. They are born dreamers, and they view the world through completely innocent eyes. Then society, the world, and human interaction work together and begin to alter our brilliant minds. We start to see the world differently, and we unknowingly create this fear as adults. Sure, as we get older, more risks are involved, we may be supporting a family, and we think about the long-term damage that could happen before we think about the greatness that can happen.

Have you ever talked yourself right out of doing something great that you know in your heart is the right move? You know you have the capacity, capability, and brainpower to complete it, but you were unsure about how it would come together for you? You've thought through every single scenario but remained stuck because you are afraid to fail, or you worry you can't afford to fail? I want you to look at your risk and then really focus on your reward. No journey is a smooth, paved road, but if your dream works out for the best, is your reward still greater than the risk? If it's a "Yes," then let me ask you again, what do you fear? What comes to mind is, "O ye of little faith" Matthew 8:26 KJV. Where is your faith? Do you have faith in the size of a mustard seed? Or are you relying upon yourself, rather than on God, to carry you through your journey? If your faith has wavered, I challenge you to spend time with God and ask for guidance and provision for the vision placed inside you. It may take time, but it's important to intentionally cling to God so He may make His vision for you plain.

If you are counting on yourself to carry you through your journey, I can share with you the outcome right now, before you even begin. You cannot do it on your own. You need help! Our lives weren't created to maneuver through the challenges alone, even when we feel as if we are isolated with no friends or family to call, God is still present. I admit, there have been times when I couldn't feel God, even in the quiet moments, and I'll share a few of those vulnerable moments with you. In the end, He still turned it around for my good, which means He was there all along. So, once again, I ask you, what are you afraid of during this season of your life? The dream that is poignant in your heart in a positive way and revealing itself to you as you have been reading is waiting for you.

Pensive: What have you not pursued because of your fears? What is something you can do today to take a small step in pushing towards your dreams?

_____

_____

_____

_____

_____

_____

_____

_____

_____

_____

_____

_____

_____

_____

_____

_____

_____

_____

_____

Perfection

Perfection is a false sense of being your authentic self; it's also unachievable. For any Perfectionist reading this, the statement above was tough to read. I get it because I have always struggled with perfectionism. Today, I continue to retrain my mind's unhealthy habits of constantly trying to improve my best. My perfectionism started in elementary school. I can remember my parents pressuring me to have all A's and B's on my report card, and it would be the best icing on the cake if I brought home straight A's. In their eyes, they were only trying to inspire me by pushing me to do my best. I do not fault them at all; however, mentally, it created this idealism of being Perfect. I worried about earning a C or below, even if it was my best, and developed a warped expectation of who I had to be the perfect daughter. I struggled with math growing up, and even today, I do not handle the budget in my household; when I did, I failed. Math was always a struggle in school, but internally I knew I had to do whatever was needed not to bring home a bad grade.

The feeling of not bringing home anything less than a B (and it needed to be a high B at that) cultivated a "win by any means necessary" mentality in me. Thankfully, this mentality never caused me to step on others to get where I wanted. That spirit has never been in my DNA, and I honestly despise sad individuals who move through society in this way. Unfortunately, I have too many stories to share where I have seen or felt like the stepping stone for others to climb the corporate ladder. I can share they are nowhere you want to be, and it didn't get them as far as they thought they should be when you think of how many people they put down to get there.

Instead, the win by any means necessary mentality meant always positioning myself in places to win. In action, this looked like being a "teacher's pet" from elementary through high school, going to my professor's office hours in college, and going above and beyond in my corporate job to be seen as outstanding. The personal sacrifices I have made throughout my life were uncalled for and caused me plenty of undue stress.

Going to therapy helped me discover the depth of my perfectionism and the unhealthy habits it created. Perfectionism has been the leading cause of my self-imposed anxiety, comparisonitis, self-worth struggles, overzealous moments of pursuing individual success that is not a part of my God-given plan, and exhaustion from being burned out. In therapy, I've explored that not being perfect is normal, and on a spiritual level, my perfectionism could be seen as me depending too much on my abilities and not allowing God to carry me through the journey. Previously, I would call on God to help me when I hit a roadblock in my journey rather than allowing God to be with me before I even started whatever it was I wanted to do. Even today, I still find myself falling short on this, but I can now catch myself earlier in the process, which shows progress, not perfection, as the goal.

Pensive: Has your personality blocked you from being your best? Have you built a wall so tall and so strong to protect yourself that you are now not your true authentic self? Who caused you to build those walls? What can you do to begin to break those walls down?

_____
_____
_____
_____
_____
_____
_____
_____
_____
_____
_____
_____
_____
_____
_____
_____

Proficient

In the Latin dialect, the term, Alma Mater, is derived from two words that translate to "nourishing mother." Clark Atlanta University (CAU) served as a nourishing mother to my young adulthood. It took me under her wing at eighteen years old after leaving what I knew my entire life in Houston, Texas. My five years at CAU was a self-discovery journey; I had space and time to develop who I wanted to be. When I talk about who and what I wanted to be, I'm not talking Professionally but more so personally. I explored my true inner spirit and was surrounded by friends, faculty, and staff who loved me just because I was worthy of being loved.

Attending a Historically Black College and University (HBCU) was one of the best decisions in and for my life. The lifelong friendships that were created, the connections that were made, the life lessons, the good and tough moments, the knowledge that was shared, the care that you felt, the net that was there to catch you when you fell short, there simply isn't another place in the world like Clark Atlanta University. I had the very best time of my life (let's just say the blood of Jesus covered me) while learning who I am as a Black woman. Our two mottos, "I'll find a way or make one." – Atlanta University, and "Culture for Service," -Clark College, become a part of your DNA. You realize that everything you do is for those who come before you and for others coming after you; you push to make the world better than the day before.

The most impressive skill I learned is how to work a room when I need to learn the information at hand. I learned how to captivate any room I walk into with the confidence that I have the awareness, understanding, poise, and knowledge for whatever the room or group is discussing. While at CAU, I learned the skills I need to get wherever I aspire to be.

As I matriculated through CAU, I was affirmed of my inner beauty. I was pushed to be the very best version of myself daily. After being accepted into the best sorority ever, Alpha Kappa Alpha Sorority Inc. "Sweet" Alpha Pi chapter, I gained an even deeper understanding of myself, and my community expanded considerably. The love that I have for my Line Sisters is as if they are blood and we were birthed from the womb of the same mother. We are all so unique in our own ways, but we learned to move as one, and we remain in sync even over ten years later. Our love and connection still run deep in our veins. We are each other's support systems, best friends, Maids and Matrons of honors, God Parents to each other's children, confidants when we are going through painful moments, secret holders, friends to celebrate our accomplishments with, business partners, party girls, travel besties, and share countless inside jokes that only we enjoy and understand.

My Line Sisters will always hold a very special place locked in my heart because my immediate Prophytes did a phenomenal job of bringing us together. It wasn't an easy road by far with them as my big sisters because they had such high expectations of each of us, but I am thankful for what they did to pour into our journey. My Line Sisters and I would not be as close as we are if it weren't for what they did to us and for us in our process. The Big Sisters of my undergraduate chapter have supported me with every transition during my adulthood. They provided a home away from home; they were like my bonus Aunts in a way. I would wash clothes at their home, and they would give me breaks from the café, although Wednesday fried chicken in the café was the best, and would take me out to eat at fancy restaurants. They sent home-cooked meals, gave me advice on what professors to seek out, gave me cash as a broke college student, and even took me to church with them. I will be forever thankful for all they have poured and are still pouring into me. Shaunte, Rae, Anya, Shavanda, TT, Robin, Janis, Fall 2003, Spring 2005, Spring 2007 Raven Symone, Ty'Sha, I do what I do for you all.

I majored in Early Childhood Education with a minor in Culture and Religion, and during my last year at CAU, I was required to do student teaching where I would go into Atlanta Public Schools and get a feel for teaching. Surprisingly, I quickly realized that I actually didn't enjoy the kids at all. My entire childhood, I always wanted to be a teacher, and now that I had the opportunity, it was not what I imagined. There I was, in year five of my undergraduate studies, poised and ready to graduate, and I suddenly discovered that I hated the very thing I had come to do. To say I felt lost would be an understatement.

To remedy this feeling of confusion and uncertainty, I decided that I would go to the University's career fair to hopefully discover a different route. From this one career fair, I received three incredible offers! I chose the career my Big Sister Janis (class of 1985) sponsored from her company. She set me up for success right from the beginning. She coached me to excel at the company she knew so much about, but she also told me when I was wrong and encouraged me to do better. This is the spirit of giving back that is now ingrained in me because I know and understand the importance of receiving guidance.

The professionalism and personal skills I gained under the supervision of my dear HBCU Clark Atlanta University are unmatched, and I am forever indebted to this institution which gave me so much. I encourage every brown child to attend any HBCU, but the best place to call home is 223 James P. Brawley Atlanta, Georgia 30314. Black and Brown students have the heavy load of growing in a world that is not rooting for them. There is plenty of time to get your fair share of life knockouts in the world. Use your time during your undergraduate years to prepare yourself for what the world has to offer. Our schools were made and designed for us to thrive in our own environments, but they also teach you how to make your own space in a world that was not created for us to succeed and to not only survive but be of excellence.

Pensive: Have you been on your self-discovery journey? What did you discover? How did you change? How have you changed since you discovered yourself? Are you still evolving? In what ways do you see yourself changing? How can you surround yourself with people who love you unconditionally?

_____
_____
_____
_____
_____
_____
_____
_____
_____
_____
_____
_____
_____
_____
_____
_____

Promising Partnership

Can you describe a relationship that is beautiful beyond what we can imagine, a safe place for all of your hurt, pain, frustrations, disappointments, the home to your vulnerability, the birthplace of joint fruitfulness, but has the potential to be abused, mishandled, misguided, neglected, and stagnate with no harvest of fruit being produced? I call this relationship MARRIAGE.

We've all heard the saying, "Marriage is hard." In the beginning, you might ask yourself how anything can be difficult when you're spending the rest of your life with the love of your life? Well, let me share with you although I heard many terrifying stories and had even seen for myself what marriage could be, good and bad, I just had so much hope that my marriage would be different.

I met Anthony Moore of South Carolina at Clark Atlanta University through a mutual friend in our first year of College in October 2007 at the age of 18. We didn't think much about each other as we were exploring our new worlds away from home, and Anthony made it very clear he did not want to be in a relationship. I suppose he was the typical male at CAU, where the ratio was 5:1 males to females. I think it's fair to say the boys definitely were able to have their cake and eat too! We reconnected over summer break 2008, and we began to date one another and build a solid friendship.

As with many college relationships, we also had our struggles. Everything that you can think might happen to teenagers trying to be adults happened to us. It was a complete movie. From cheap dates at Waffle House to order the T-bone steak, me getting extra help off Ant's Spanish homework, Ant transferring to USC to be closer to home and leaving me at CAU creating a difficult long-distance relationship, cheating on each other in college, an abortion my last year of college, living together after college while still operating on our schedules, lost jobs, all the way to getting married while having unrealistic expectations and unhealed wombs that showed up in different ways in our marriage.

We each brought our insecurities and immaturities into a pipe dream full of potential and hope into a new relationship. I've always had a vivid imagination, and as a little girl, I knew I wanted to be married. I knew wedding colors, cake designs, and I had it all planned without a groom. When the groom came, I was still focused on the wedding and not the marriage. That's mistake number one for a healthy marriage.

In my dreams, I always saw this picture-perfect marriage, also known as mistake number two. Anthony and I dated for seven years before he asked for my hand in marriage, and then we spent a year enjoying our engagement. In May

all of that we did, we know we never want to be back in that space again. In order to move to the Connected category, within our first year of marriage, Anthony and I came up with rules that we would follow until death. We share these 10 tips with everyone in prayer that they help another couple as much as they have helped us.

1. *Christ must stay as our cornerstone in our marriage.* We want to grow together in Christ. In real life, this looks like us doing a weekly devotional, attending church, being active members in our church's marriage ministry, and attending Life Group together.

2. *Commit to each other.* Commit as if you and your spouse are in a locked room with no windows and the only key to the room was ground to dust. It's only you, your spouse, and God. There is no way in or out, so you have to stay in to work it out. Another way I like to put this is, don't let devils and the enemy in your marriage. An enemy is any THING or PERSON that is not pushing you towards your spouse.

3. *Seek support for your marriage as preventative care.* We are not meant to walk through life alone. A healthy marriage needs a community to not only survive but to thrive. You need other couples who support your marriage and to let you know when you need correction.

Don't wait until you and your spouse are to your wit's end to get the support your marriage needs.

4. *Communicate in the way your spouse understands.* This takes work as we all communicate differently and understand tones, facial expressions, and body language differently based on our unique past experiences. Anthony and I finally realized that after a disagreement, he needs time to process his thoughts before giving me a full response. I used to be so confused that I would have a mouth full to say, and the response I would get in return would be "ok." We finally had a tough conversation to understand what our needs are in tough moments. You may have to go through trial and error to figure out the best way of communicating with each other.

5. *Remain friends and date.* Whatever you and your spouse did before marriage that was fun for you both, continue to do this. Be open to trying new things together as you will grow to like different things. Become a student of your spouse. No one should know your spouse better than you. This takes vulnerability that is created through close intimacy.

6. *Compromise, compromise, compromise.* It's no longer about who is right or wrong, it's about what is right for you both. In really tough moments of marriage,

remember you are fighting an issue or problem together; you're not fighting each other. Stay focused on the problem, not the character of your spouse. Don't judge or draw a line in the sand around what you will or won't put up within a marriage. You will be surprised at how much you will need to compromise when you're married. If you are the person who always has something to say and it's always about what you 'aren't going to do,' you are not ready to get married.

7. *Let God lead you through your marriage.* When you get frustrated, and you will get frustrated, call on God first. Then get quiet and listen to what He has in His will for you to do. This action takes obedience, but I am a living witness that it works. When I am upset, frustrated, or disappointed with Anthony, the first thing I do is pray and wait for God. I used to be hurtful with my words and just take matters into my own hands... which led us further away from God and further away from one another.

8. *Try teamwork.* The best teams in sports like basketball, football, and hockey, and within corporate environments, all have a few things in common, trust, accountability, shared vision, quality time together, and respect for each other's strengths and weaknesses. Just because I can do something doesn't mean I should

do it. I remember a time when Anthony and I struggled badly with finances. We would butt heads about the budget constantly. I was doing the budget at the time, but it wasn't my strength. I finally relinquished doing the budget, and what a world of difference it made. We went from having a small savings and always scrambling to pay all of our bills at the last minute, to paying all of our bills well ahead of time, plus a very healthy savings account. Relinquishing control and supporting Anthony as he works in his area of strength has helped our finances flourish.

9. *Forgive fast, extend grace, and be kind.* Your spouse is still human. Mistakes will still happen and so will disappointments. When you understand how much God forgives you and how He so generously extends grace and mercy to you, it will become easier for you to do the same for your spouse.

10. *Choose love daily and stay acutely in tune emotionally with one another.* Love is a choice; you can choose to love your spouse daily even when you don't feel like loving them. There will be days when you don't feel like loving your spouse. Here is the real deal, there may come a time when your spouse doesn't choose to love you, be kind to you, and extend grace to you. It is still your responsibility to govern your actions and do so

even when your spouse chooses differently. Love is truly seen when it is sacrificial love, just as Jesus sacrificed Himself on the cross for you and me.

I've been married for four years, but in that time, God has allowed me to experience many obstacles using a critical eye which has been key to supporting others in their marriages. I've learned that you must be intentional. Be intentional with your prayer time together, fun time together, your friendship to one another, and never let go of Christ's divine love. God can and will cover your marriage if you ask Him to. Invite God in so that your marriage can see the fruit that you can only obtain with Him in the center. Marriage is one of the only relationships that can adequately mirror and model to others the glorious ways in which Christ loved the church. Be the marriage where others can see the love of Christ.

Pensive: Do you have the partnership you desire? If you are still single, what do you desire in a person? How can you prepare for your partnership? How can you be a better partner?

_____

_____

_____

_____

_____

_____

_____

_____

_____

_____

_____

_____

_____

_____

_____

_____

_____

_____

_____

Privilege

"Don't be upset if you want to play with everyone and everyone doesn't choose to play with you back. Just go find new people to play with." - Vera J. Jessie (my mother)

It was 1998 when I begged my parents to take me out of my all-Black, Christian private school to start at my zoned public elementary school. My parents were very hesitant to move me because my learning needs were being catered to with a challenge and love but more so because the teachers and students at the Christian school were my family.

I was born and raised in the suburbs of Houston, Texas, to a middle-class family. I was the second (and last) child and the only little girl. My mother is very religious, and we were in church multiple times a week. Sunday service was oftentimes more than one service back to back. We attended Wednesday night Bible study, choir rehearsals, usher board meetings, and the list goes on. Each summer was filled with traveling to different states across the country to spend a week and a half with our church affiliation to worship as a group and participate in the Bible Quiz. That's right, there was even a Bible Quiz, and it was a pretty big deal to defend your geographic location!

My Father, affectionately known as Papa, was not religious and never understood the small church setting, so he found a megachurch that was a lot faster-paced than our old school small church. As a result, my brother and I were involved in two distinctly different churches growing up. Needless to say, whether we wanted to or not, we didn't have a choice not to get to know God.

My Civil Rights era, Baby Boomer parents only knew to be cautious with other ethnic groups of people because they had seen too much. My mother, born and raised in Brandon, Mississippi, was among the first group of Black children to integrate her high school. She was the 1st Black cheerleader and continued to break barriers on the basketball team. Papa was born and raised in Buffalo, New York. Although we were taught in grade school that the North was much better than the South when it came to black and white experiences, from his stories, it really didn't seem too different.

As an adult, who over the years, has gained a plethora of experiences by my own account, I can see why my parents thought it was important to shield my brother and me from the harsh reality that many of us in the black community face every single day. Now being a parent myself, my husband and I are determined to help this country be better for ourselves but, more importantly, for our daughter. We can all help by showing Christ to everyone through unconditional love. This means loving people who are different from us, who have a different point of view than me, even the people who hate us for our skin color. Our job is to still love unconditionally.

It's also imperative to us to create diverse environments. In our society, it is easy and natural to stay in what feels comfortable. It takes work to insert yourself into various unfamiliar settings, but this is where magic can truly happen. Building relationships with individuals that may not have the same understanding as you is critical. Hearts, minds, even entire communities can change because of the actions of just one person, but long-lasting change is most likely to come through relationships. It's extremely hard to give hate to someone when you walk through life with them. You gain a special understanding when you hear their experiences and see for yourself who someone is, rather than depending on secondhand information or media sources. We must be intentional in everything we do. From seeking out different types of Baby/Barbie dolls so that your child feels seen, all the way to creating safe spaces for our children to play, learn, and simply enjoy being a kid.

Finally, let's talk about racism. Racism is a frequent topic of conversation in many Black homes. We speak about it because we have to prepare our children for a country and world that was not built for them. Talking to your children about embracing people who are different from you is an integral part of training your children to have empathy. Let's learn for ourselves the full history of America, and let's commit to teaching our children what the history books don't share. By sharing American history (and not Black history because Black history is American history), generations can change right around your dinner table. Who wouldn't want to be a part of changing the world?

As a 31-year old Black woman protesting for the same things my parents and grandparents protested for is disappointing. My maternal grandfather marched right along with Dr. Martin Luther King, Jr. for the exact same thing that I have been marching for since my freshman year of college. It's a bittersweet feeling. I'm bitter, and I find myself asking, "Why now?"

Was it not enough to witness the murders of Emmitt Till (1955), or Sean Bell (2006) on his wedding day, or Tamir Rice (2014), who was only twelve years old, or Michael Brown (2014), or Eric Gardner (2014), or Sandra Bland (2015), or Freddie Gray (2015) Philando Castile (2016), or Terence Crutcher (2016), or Jocques Clemmons (2017), or Stephon Clark (2018), or Antwan Rose (2018), or Botham Jean (2019), or Derrick Scott (2020)? What about the most recent tragedies of today with Breonna Taylor (2020), Ahmaud Arbery (2020), Rayshard Brooks (2020), and George Floyd (2020)?

Unfortunately, this is not even the complete list. There are way too many people to name who have lost their lives at the hands of someone who should have been protecting them. I'm thankful that there seems to be a revolution starting as more and more people become aware, but I hate that it took so many people to lose their lives in order for some people in this country to wake up.

My husband Anthony put my frustration into perspective a week ago when he shared, "We don't condemn people when it takes them longer to come to Christ. We just jump in, help, teach and welcome them in becoming Christians. We should treat people the same who are now jumping in and being catalysts for change." Although, in my opinion, it has taken too long for change to come, I am grateful the type of change happening right now is a heart change because once our hearts are changed, we see the word, truth, with a cross for the t.

I'm proud to educate and continue the conversations about race with anyone who will hear. In our black communities, and even inside the walls of our churches, we discuss race all the time, but we do ourselves a disservice because we are the only ones hearing it. We have to continue to build multi-ethnic churches so these messages can be shared from a Christ-led perspective and with a heart for how He intended this world to be.

Pensive: How did you grow up? What were your parents' views on integration? In what ways does

racial injustice affect you? What can you do about it?

_____

_____

_____

_____

_____

_____

_____

_____

_____

_____

_____

_____

_____

_____

_____

_____

_____

_____

_____

_____

Politics

I have never cared about how others identified politically. Independent, Democrat, Republican, I never cared because, truth be told, I have a shared identity with all of them on different topics. What I do care about is the candidate. If you support someone who is disrespectful without remorse, has no desire to lead in an inclusive way, and is ignorant to the knowledge given, or refuses to find it out for him/herself that is where I have the problem.

I have personally been a victim of discrimination in the workplace and through my daily life on several occasions, and as a Black woman, I've even been racially profiled. If you have ever been in those positions and know what this feels like, it's not something you would knowingly do to someone else. A great leader is a great leader, no matter where you put them, because a characteristic of a leader is someone who adapts even if they have never performed the task or been in a particular situation.

I think it is often forgotten that America, as a country, doesn't have one official religion. It is not Christianity, nor was it fully built off of Christian culture. Despite what some may claim, uniquely American events like slavery, discrimination, immigration laws, and tax laws are not based on true Christian belief. Religion is played when it's convenient for politicians. Although I am a Christian, I believe, if America is supposed to be the land of the free, you have to allow people to be free. As much as I want everyone to experience the love of God through Jesus Christ coming to save us all, it is also not for me to push my religion on anyone. The best thing that I can do to be a disciple of Christ is to engage and connect with people, build relationships with them, and love them. The goal is for others to see the love of Christ through you, how you move, how you're able to still have fun but be a great person and do the right thing even when no one is looking (because someone is always looking).

I think as a country, America has done a very poor job creating equality across the board. If you are not a white male in America, there have been at least one or two statements in the constitution indicating that it was acceptable for you to be discriminated against. This is why voting is so important. When I vote both locally and nationally, I vote with people who are less fortunate, most vulnerable, and whose voices remain unheard. I vote with my daughter and my 95-year-old great aunt in mind.

I truly had a change of heart when it comes to certain topics that have turned political such as abortion and welfare. I was using birth control when Anthony and I found out I was pregnant in 2012. We made the difficult decision to choose abortion because I knew I wouldn't have the support to give my child the best I could. It was my senior year in undergrad, and I didn't have a job lined up. Ant was in South Carolina finishing his program and still had another year left. My parents were in Houston, and I had very few family members in Atlanta that would have supported us. I was very uncertain about the future. At the time, it felt like the only option to be able to have a better life for our future children.

I was the one to make the call, and I thank God for Ant because he didn't pressure me either way. I made the decision, and I knew he would do his best to support me no matter what decision I made. The issue I have with pro-life and anti-abortion movements is, what is the alternative if you get pregnant? Take a chance to live in poverty? Or give the baby up for adoption? We all know that the foster care system is not up to par, and I, despite my admiration for others who do, would not willingly do that. This was the best choice to set my future family and me up for success.

For years, I stuck to my decision and would share my story without remorse. As I grew, guilt slowly started to unveil itself. I ended up graduating from my university and, rather immediately, getting a job making a little over $60k. Although that would have still been tough to swing with daycare and baby needs, I could have made it. I now make double what I started with, am married to the love of my life, and we have a very comfortable lifestyle. I battle with the decision now because, in hindsight, maybe I just did not have enough faith.

• • •

I often ask myself, was I that selfish? I had always thought of this being a selfless act; my thought pattern was, "How can you knowingly bring babies into the world and not be able to give them your best?" I now realize that I relied on myself and didn't put my faith where it should have been, in what God could do. I didn't include God at all in my decision. I have since asked God for forgiveness, and I now spend time showing others the love Christ showed me no matter what choice they make. I would never judge anyone who made the same decision I made, and I also intentionally support women who bring children into this world who need the extra support that I didn't think I would've had. God's grace is everlasting, and I'm so thankful for his mercy towards me.

• • •

Pensive: How does your religious view impact your political view? Do you see them as the same? Have you ever judged someone, then ended up in a similar situation?

_____
_____
_____
_____
_____
_____
_____
_____
_____
_____
_____
_____
_____
_____
_____
_____
_____
_____
_____
_____
_____

Proponent

"Great friends are hard to come by," is a saying we have all heard. This statement has never rung true for me. I have always had a great reputation for choosing great friends. I saw my mama have great friends growing up in Texas, she had her core group back home in Mississippi, her core group of co-workers, and her community grew from there. In Houston, we grew up away from family, so friends were our family; they were aunts, cousins, and vice versa. "The Girls," as my mama affectionately called them, would get together about once a month at someone's home, and they would play cards and have margaritas. We knew their families, and we even knew their extended family. We were all family. Seeing my mama have such good friends influenced me in how I cultivated my friendships as a young adult.

Friends are so important. Friends can carry you when you simply can't push yourself. My friends have supported me in more ways than I can count. They are the girls I can always depend upon to tell me the truth even when I'm wrong, give me sound advice, encourage me, listen to me complain without judgment. They know when I need a pick-me-up, they will do anything for me, and I know they have my back. We've been through tough seasons together but also prosperous and flourishing seasons too.

• • •

Friendships are truly a gift from God. Life is not meant to get through alone. Sure, you may have lonely moments, but knowing you have a good friend is simply good for your mental health. I've never shared this list before, so this is a *Leslie A. J. Moore Exclusive*, on how to choose the best friends for yourself, because I think this is imperative for you to know.

1. *Be friends with people who connect to your inner being.* A lot of people are friends with the people who they aspire to be, but they may not truly be able to connect to who you are because you both are not giving your authentic self.

2. *Time doesn't matter.* You will grow, you will learn more, and evolve into a better person. Just because you are no longer connecting with a friend doesn't mean you have to drop them. Always cheer for them and let them know that.

3. *Engage with friends who aren't afraid to tell you the truth.* It feels good to hear you're doing good all the time, but if you get this feedback when you have fallen short, this is not helpful to your growth.

4. *Surround yourself with people from other age groups.* I have friends that are in different age categories. Several could be my parents and a few,

my children if I had started having kids at sixteen. A diverse group gives you a range of opportunities to learn. You will discover what is important to them while being a mentor or a mentee.

5. *Trust and vulnerability are imperative in any relationship, but it's critical to friendships on both ends.* As with any relationship, a friendship doesn't work if it's one-sided. If I am the only one spilling my beans to a friend and I am hardly ever able to listen to your side, that situation can become one-sided. Even being able to share your wins with friends is important. I would hate to see my friend announcing something special on social media, and it's my first time hearing about it.

6. *Friendships often fail because there is no grace included.* Let me ask you this when a friend does something that you don't like, are you typically ready to cut them off and chalk it up to "the principle"? If so, I get it. I've been at that point before, too. Rather than immediately cutting someone off, can you think back and honestly say that you have set appropriate expectations with your friend? Did you share with them the type of friend you expect to be to them? When you found yourself in the wrong, did you sincerely apologize

to them? When you feel they have wronged you, did you tell them? Did you act as if nothing happened? Did you ghost them? I suggest taking a moment to instead show grace to them, set the expectations, and move forward.

7. *Hold your friends accountable for what they said they would do and expect to do the same in return.* Also, push them to be the best version of themselves. If they are their best, this will indirectly and sometimes even directly support you in being your best.

Within my group of friends, there is nothing that, collectively, we haven't been through. I know that I can always count on at least one of them to share a similar experience. I have created an incredible community of friends. My first group of friends is seven amazing women who we have all seen each other through major life milestones. They consist of my first cousin Ashley, my oldest best friend from high school, Tiara, and five of my Line Sisters, Olivia, Katrina, Victoria, DeJonique, and Khemari. All seven were the Matrons/Maids of Honor in my wedding. I didn't have any bridesmaids because they all meant that much to me. They are different in every way that can be imagined, but we all get along as if we are all the best of friends.

My next group is my 4ever4life group. We were each other's rock while we were all at the same company with different positions but dealing with the same discrimination as black women while carrying our departments on our backs without recognition. We each had our struggles personally and professionally. It has felt as if we've been rocking together for a lifetime. We were able to write this book together!

Finally, I can't miss out on calling on my sorority sisters, who are not my best friends but are pretty close to knowing much about me, but without every detail, and my church family would be put into this same category. As you may have picked up on, I don't meet many strangers.

I understand that everyone may not be blessed with a family of friends as I have, and you may have even been burned in the past with friends. I also understand how this can build a wall whether you have wanted to or not. I want to share that I, too, have had to cut friends off after I noticed habits that didn't connect to my inner being. If they continue to wrong you, show them the patterns you have observed through a conversation when you are not angry. Give your friend a chance to change and show you that they want to be a good friend to you. If you feel it's time to move on from this friendship, be direct but polite. Just because you are moving from the friendship doesn't mean you don't still love them. It also doesn't mean that you don't wish them well in all of their endeavors. Share with them that you still love them and you wish them well, but you will cheer for them from afar. I have had this conversation a few times, and there has been no love lost.

Pensive: Who are your friends? Have you been a good friend? In this season, what do you need most from your friends? How have your friends pushed you? Do you have any ex-friends that you need to apologize to?

_____
_____
_____
_____
_____
_____
_____
_____
_____
_____
_____
_____
_____
_____
_____
_____
_____
_____
_____

<u>Peroration</u>

I've poured out my heart and all I have to give of my thirty-one years of life. I can't guarantee this is my last published writing because I pray I have at least fifty more years of experience to go. If you don't take anything else from my section of the book, I want you to know you are here for a reason. All of the things that you have deemed as pointless or unnecessary to your life's story, remember, you are only seeing small sections of a beautiful masterpiece.

Your life may not always go as you've planned it, but it can go exactly as it should according to God's will. When I think about all of the difficult and messed-up things I've gone through, I am still able to turn around and give God the glory. There will be seasons when you feel you have been overlooked. You might be jumping up and down trying to be noticed, whether it's personally or professionally, I'm here to share with you to get still and listen to God's small whispers. God thinks about you more than the grains of sand near an ocean, yes you! He cares for you, and even when we can't feel Him close, He's still right there beside you because He will never leave you nor forsake you (*see* Deuteronomy 31:6).

There will be times when it feels as if your faith is being tested. Those were my toughest seasons. I felt it would be easier to just let go of God's unchanging hand. Even in those tough seasons, you've got to keep the faith. I remember when I was told my job would be shipped to India. After over seven years at the company, my role as a Process Training Manager, the role that just a few months earlier I had decided was no longer a good fit for me because I was ready for a new challenge, was being outsourced.

I went on Maternity Leave in February 2019, and in June 2019, while still on leave, I was informed that my role was being eliminated and transferred to India. They shared that I had a job until my date of November 1st and that I had several services to support me through this transition that I could use. In a way, I knew this day was coming, but I didn't think it would be soon or honestly affect me. I, of course, called my husband Ant to tell him that HR just called me, and his exact words were, "It's fine, I already did the budget without your salary." At this point, I became so grateful for a husband that was money savvy and knew how to save well (I do a great job of spending).

Between the time of knowing my job was eliminated and me going back to work, Ant and I looked into me being a stay-at-home mom. If you know me, you know that this was a dream of mine since I was a little girl! But something was missing. I hadn't accomplished all that I wanted to do in the corporate world and knew I wanted to share my gifts with more people. So I declined to stay home and set out to find a new path.

I went back to work in July but was on a mission to find a new job outside of the company, with Ant's voice in the back of my head, "Don't settle for any job, only apply to things you want to do." This statement that Ant constantly told me was a game-changer. I took my search seriously, and if the job description didn't speak to me or the company didn't line up with my principles and things important to me, I didn't apply.

I'm sure I applied to well over 200 jobs. I got countless calls from recruiters, I spoke to several hiring managers for first-round interviews, and I went on numerous final interviews. I can't even tell you the number of denial emails I received, but with each denial, I affirmed to myself, "With every No, I'm closer to Yes." I applied to so many jobs that there was nothing else out there I could apply to.

I finally moved to the final round of this one position that I knew I was PERFECT for. I went to the interview; I did a stellar job, and I knew the job was mine! It was on the fourteenth floor of a beautiful building in uptown Charlotte. A week later, I got the generic denial email, and that knocked the wind out of me! I was devastated, I cried for hours, I was pissed! How could they not choose me? Do they know who they just denied!?! On top of that, it was a generic form email! After spending the day with you and spending $50 on parking? "Y'all gotta give me more than this," my thoughts screamed!

• • •

Let me show you how God works, though. Earlier that week, before my denial letter came from the job I just knew I had, my position at Walmart was extended to the new year! Talk about PROVISION, and when I tell you, God knows his child! This confirmed to me that God has me and to chill out! I continued to look for jobs, but my mindset began to shift and grow as my family joined our church Transformation Church in Indian Land, South Carolina. I promise, EVERY SINGLE Sunday, my toes were being stepped on, and my mind expanded, talk about conviction! I was at such peace with what God had for me and just knew he would meet every need and more.

I made it to another final interview, but as I shared before, my mindset had changed. No longer was I overly anxious. I was calm but excited. Get this, this company was in the same building as the job I knew I had gotten but on the twenty-second floor (my line number). I met and interviewed eleven different people and I had such a phenomenal time, I didn't want to leave! After all eleven people interviewed me I thought this was it. I was in. Nope! I had a culture interview just two days later! I appreciated this as I think more companies should invest in this strategy, and coming from a company that didn't do this final interview, it showed me how important this was.

On the Tuesday before Thanksgiving, I got the call that I got the job! I was elated, and I literally could only thank God. I share all of this to say that you may feel overlooked, going through struggles can make you feel worthless, you may start having anxiety. That's human nature. I'm here to tell you to keep the faith. You are all that and a bag of chips. You were created for greatness, and I want you to know your worth comes from above, not from a paycheck, status, your kids, or what you have obtained in life. Get you some encouraging friends that can build you up during this time, and BE YOUR TRUE SELF! I now know I didn't get the job on the fourteenth floor because of my personality, and at the end of the day, I'm ok with that because I want to be my authentic self every day.

Fast forward to COVID-19, and after four months on my new job, I got furloughed. I received notice on the same day I was up at 4:30 am to put in work before Arley, my baby girl got up, the same day, I shared publicly on social media how much I enjoyed my job and felt the work I did was meaningful. To say I was disappointed was an understatement. I wasn't upset with the company because I understood. I was in the parking/transportation industry, so there was an immediate impact when COVID-19 hit, and we all began working from home. I was upset with the United States government administration and officials who knew the impact and magnitude of what COVID-19 could be and failed to plan. I'm still upset that we as citizens were lied to about how this could really impact our nation. I'll be the first to share that I didn't take COVID-19 seriously because in the beginning, it was "like the flu" and nothing was shut down, so in my eyes, that meant it was time to shop!

I was also frustrated with myself for being in a similar position that I just left with my last company. I simply couldn't understand how this was happening to me again! I immediately started a grieving process and I just couldn't pinpoint why I was taking this loss differently than my prior job loss. I found myself trying to figure out what my next job was going to be. I signed up to be an Instacart shopper, and I looked into dropping off packages for Amazon. I just wanted to do something, anything! I finally told Ant what I was doing, and he was mad. He, of course, told me to chill out and sit down somewhere, use this time to rest, and find a hobby. Despite his good intentions, this only made me sadder. Even though we weren't dependent on my income, I am a helper. I feel my best when I am helping to achieve a common goal, especially in my marriage. I like bringing home a nice check and seeing us save it, invest it, pay off debts, etc., so I felt compelled to support in any way I could. I'm a ride or die.

I suppose after a few days, Ant had enough of me. We were in bed on a Sunday night, and Ant had what we call a "come to Jesus" talk with me. At this time, I was still feeling waves of grief as I would find myself thinking about a goal Ant and I were on schedule to achieve this year, and tears would begin to fall because I knew we would have to push a few goals back and it felt like it was my fault. I carried this weight, and I know Ant could sense all of this, and he was fed up.

During our talk, Ant said the most amazing thing that made a light bulb finally turn on for me. I was spilling my guts out to him, saying, "I can't believe it happened to me; I don't want us to get off track with our investment goals, friends and family keep saying I'll have more time with Arley, but you know that doesn't matter because regardless I always put you and her first..." I was going a mile a minute, and Ant butted in and said the simplest thing, "The best way you can help our family and me is by staying home. Keep you and Arley safe and healthy during this pandemic. Nothing else matters to me." I got it! I could have literally said, "Yes, Zaddy" (in my sexy voice).

Ant further helped me see that this was way bigger than our little family. Yes, we were affected but nowhere near the magnitude that others were, and I am so thankful for that. I became grateful to be furloughed and not laid off. At the time, it all meant the same thing but, I now realize this is a difference however, it brought the same emotions. I became thankful that if I had to be furloughed or laid off, it was during the time that the government was giving even more support than normal, and I was able to take advantage. I became thankful that Ant valued me being home taking care of our safe place and busy toddler

Arley because that's a job in itself! Most of all, I became thankful for a husband that grounds me and oftentimes saves me from myself. Ant knows me so well and is a phenomenal leader.

After four months of embracing my furlough by starting and hosting a book club, I read eight books and got involved in church more. Ant and I are now the Marriage Ministry leaders. I even learned sign language and got certified to be a life coach focusing on relationships and transitions. When the country reopened, I was then asked to come back to work in a similar role plus a pay increase! I was very grateful to go back to work, to a company that I love, and to a position that fits me. With every turn, I am excelling in what I do to always make them regret losing me for four months. I could have gone back with a chip on my shoulder or holding a grudge against what happened, but why would I do that? What would I gain? It's all about the approach and your perspective.

I shared all of this to say even if you are struggling in your faith, believe that God still has you. As the old folks would say, keep living, and I pray you see God's hand through every decision, relationship thought, and turn. Allow Him in and be grateful for your journey. Someone is wishing they were on your journey. There is always someone who has it worse than you so be grateful even on your worst days. Seek therapy on a regular basis, and I'm not talking about just talking to your friends. Go to a licensed professional and work through everything even if you feel you haven't been through enough, still go! Speak your truth unapologetically, spend time getting to know your inner being, be your authentic self no matter what feathers you ruffle, and ask God for forgiveness daily because you will miss the mark. Even still, remember He loves you and cares for you always.

Pensive: What are some situations that you can right now just give to God? What are you tired of carrying?

_____

_____

_____

_____

_____

_____

_____

_____

_____

_____

_____

_____

_____

_____

_____

_____

_____

_____

Acknowledgments

I want to acknowledge my husband for sticking and rocking with his crazy wife, who shares all of our business to help the next person. I also want to recognize the experiences I have had, good, bad, and ugly, the friends and people I have encountered, all of which have helped me to be able to write this portion of my book to share with others.

Cody

I'm a mommy to Taylor and Carter.

I'm a graduate of SCSU, a member of Delta Sigma Theta, Inc, a cohost of The Sip 6, and a lioness when it comes to family and friends. Lastly, I love music and enjoy a good cigar with a glass of bourbon.

"Rather than allowing our egos to dictate the relationship we have with others, we need to willingly eliminate the behavior of unforgiveness". Cody J.

<u>Dedication</u>

This is dedicated to the loved ones who transitioned from this earthly life and are now my angels. Grandma Katherine M. Caldwell and Soror Danielle Gregory Jackson, not understanding the importance of forgiveness while you were here has been extremely heavy at times. Losing the both of you was a painful ending. Reflecting on the happy memories propelled me to move forward with the closure I needed. Avery T. Byrd, I'm forever grateful for the last year you were amongst us. The apologies and clarity were healing, and it allows me to continue throughout life knowing we collectively made things right.

Taylor and Carter, mommy loves you both so much! Whatever experiences you face that may be uncomfortable, understand that you don't have to condone the impudent behavior of others, and you may not ever forget it. My prayer for the both of you is to live life with an open mind and heart and no feelings of resentment. Also, understand the importance of owning up to your faults and be apologetic. Finally, I hope this book expresses the importance of forgiveness and progressing without bitterness. I love you!

Mommy, how I wish you were here to guide me through life's unpredictability. I pray I continue to make you proud. I love and miss you immensely!

The Celebrity

If only I could turn back the hands of time. There are so many moments of life I would redo. God, I wish you would grant me a do-over. I sit in pain and heartbreak because there were so many moments when my ego, pride, and selfishness should have been set aside. Now I sit in hurt and regret because those moments that I once had are nonexistent. No do-overs. No apologies. Yet somehow, I have to move on in life and make the most out of it.

You know, it's amazing how life will give you a hard lesson in forgiveness. However, unforgiveness coupled with death is a harsh reality. My spirit and soul were guilty of being grudge-filled and uncompromising. With that, I paid the ultimate price for it. Death. There were people I loved who had hurt me, and I refused to let that hurt go. God gave me so many opportunities to make things right, yet, I ignored and disregarded those moments.

"Sometimes you have to experience losses for life to show you what you really want out of it. Unfortunately, people get hurt in the process". - Cody N. Jackson

In these last few years, I've learned that holding a grudge locks your heart from being in healthy relationships. The hurt forces you to dwell in the past, which ultimately doesn't allow you to move on successfully into your future. But somehow, after experiencing the death of two loved ones, my heart immediately softened due to grief and regret. These experiences allowed me to have a better relationship, the one I had I always wanted, with the love of my life.

The Journey to Forgiveness

Grandmother

I lost my grandmother in December of 2017. I was her oldest grandbaby and extremely spoiled—a replica of my mommy, my grandmother's only child. Whatever I wanted and needed, my grandmother made it happen. Even if she didn't have it, somehow, I was always blessed with whatever it was I had asked to receive. Not only was I spoiled, so were my siblings.

Sadly, our relationship took a turn that neither one of us expected. I had made a decision about my life that displeased her. I had started dating a woman. It went against her morals and how I was raised. She always put me on a pedestal, so her expectations of me were always pleasing in her and God's sight. However, that one decision I made regarding my life at the moment caused the worst rift ever in our relationship. It did not matter how happy I was or how my life had shifted from being broken-hearted to radiating with contentment. This was something we could not get past. Together, we entered a period of temporary silence. A silence I assumed would not be longstanding.

My life decision affected grandma and my paternal side of the family. My father, sister, grandmother, and aunts were extremely upset. They had even come together and attempted with my daughter's father to have her taken away from me. I was livid, and at that point in my life, they were dead to me. I couldn't understand how my family would disown and ostracize me. I've always been a great mother to my children, but because I made a decision that they did not accept because of how it would affect the family's name, my decision was dishonorable in their view. Their actions not only made me retreat from them but also from the church. I could not attend church with the very people who labeled themselves Christians but were hypercritical and faultfinding towards me. Thankfully, I still had the full support and unwavering love from other family members and friends.

"Do not judge, or you too will be judged. For in the same way you judge others, you will be judged, and with the measure you use, it will be measured to you" Matthew 7:1-2.

The silence lasted for two years and ended finally only due to her death. Even though Grandma had left voicemails for me to call her, I was too hurt and mad to return the phone calls. Now all I have are those voice mails that I still listen to periodically.

You may wonder, how is my relationship now with the other family members that were mentioned. Truthfully, there hasn't been complete healing. I am no longer as angry as I was, but the dynamic of our relationship has definitely been altered.

I completely comprehend the initial shock, and although their actions are incomprehensible, I can now move for.

Reflect: Is there someone within your family that has hurt you, or you hurt them? If so, write down the apology you expect or one you would issue. It's time to heal!

_____

_____

_____

_____

_____

_____

_____

_____

_____

_____

_____

_____

_____

_____

_____

_____

_____

_____

_____

_____

My Best Friend

In the summer of 2018, I lost someone who was once my very best friend. She was my sister. In that moment of losing my estranged friend, I knew the importance of forgiveness. I cried every day from that dreadful day to February 2019. It wasn't until her death that I realized it's imperative to forgive. Not only to set things right with her but as a way to also free me from bondage. Bondage of being grudge-hearted and my heart not being at peace. My heart was once again shattered.

I realized then that I had wasted all those years being disgruntled over something that could have been forgiven early on. See, I had shared with her something very personal to me, and she turned around and shared it with someone else. Then, of course, that person shared it. I am a very loyal person, so this hurt me to my core. I felt very betrayed, and it put us in a very negative space. In hindsight, this could have been resolved had I been receptive to hearing the why behind her actions. My biggest regret was allowing death to be my eye-opener.

The most important piece of forgiveness is releasing yourself of anything that could potentially hinder you from moving forward. I have an amazing circle that prayed for me and was there whenever I needed them. There were two people especially, who assisted with helping me attain the closure I needed to accept her death. They listened, never judged, and shared things with me to encourage me to move forward without a guilty heart. Although I learned difficult lessons, I'm thankful that I finally acknowledged the importance of forgiveness. Unknowingly, death was swiftly approaching once again.

Reflect: Forgiveness is imperative. It opens your heart to receive so much more. How did your life change once you forgave someone?

_____

_____

_____

_____

_____

_____

_____

_____

_____

_____

_____

_____

_____

_____

_____

_____

_____

_____

_____

_____

_____

_____

The Final Blow

Once my heart opened up, I incurred all types of blessings. Most importantly, it opened my heart up to be open to having a mature co-parenting relationship and friendship with my son's father. For that, I'm forever grateful. You see, many obstacles had obstructed our early relationship. There was a lot of hurt from his infidelity and pain from our past. For years, callous talks, petty feuds, and even an overnight stay in jail hindered us from being productive co-parents. However, we had finally gotten to the point where we conducted ourselves as adults. We communicated openly and candidly. We no longer allowed our disagreements to linger on and on. We had truly grown! Who would've thought we could be at a place where we could be friends?

The one incident that occurred between the two of us happened on September 23, 2017, which I'm sure a lot of my Chester people remember but maybe not quite the details. We had a huge argument in his front yard regarding child support. I needed the money, which turned into him trash-talking, which then led to a domestic dispute. Although I didn't make contact with him, when the police arrived, and the community gathered around, they rallied together and placed the blame on me. You guessed it! I went to jail. I stayed up all night and called my sister and KC. As I sat in that cold cell, all I could think about was I wanted him to suffer because I couldn't understand how he could send his son's mother to jail. You talk about the ultimate heartbreak! I hated him. The agony and pain from the person you once trusted your heart with is a different level of numbness.

I'll tell anyone until this day…Don't do anything to go to jail because it's cold in there! So, I'm sure it was surprising for many to see our relationship had turned from constant bickering to becoming best friends. Sadly, we used to have Facebook on fire with ALL of our drama. So that's all people knew.

As I previously stated, I had already lost two loved ones from whom I had been estranged. The state of my early relationship with my son's father was turbulent. Thankfully, before the dreaded day of September 14th, his untimely passing, he and I had finally made peace. Understanding and clarity were the foundation of our new friendship. Forgiveness and mutual understanding had been discovered.

No relationship is perfect, but considering where we had been and how we had grown, WE WERE PERFECT! We had finally learned to speak like adults. If I was upset, he didn't allow it to linger. The relationship we had previously was sometimes debilitating. I could not understand how someone I gave my all to would hurt me the way that he had. When someone knowingly hurts you and has heard the cries and pleading, it is hard to process the why. Why would you bruise the heart of the person who loves you unconditionally? It was difficult for me to process during our relationship and even afterward.

Nonetheless, we were in love. Although we had endured so much pain in our past, once we accepted responsibility for our actions and offered apologies, our past was just that, our past. Therefore, if we decided to bring anything up regarding our past, we listened, explained our actions without justifications or excuses, apologized, and moved on.

The thing that is so interesting about writing about forgiveness, I have said time and time again that I could write a book about our relationship. Although there were strenuous moments and incidents that I did not think I would ever recover from, the beautiful times are what I now choose to reflect on. It's funny how even in your most strained relationships, you learn the biggest lessons. If it wasn't for forgiveness, I would not have been able to move on productively. I would again be drowned in grief and regret.

The Stages of Forgiveness

Healing in Forgiveness

Forgiveness is healing. Just think about how it affects your life, spiritually, emotionally, and physically. Forgiveness is important for your mental health and well-being. The negative thoughts you harvest within affect your mental health. Think about it, have you ever sat and thought about a situation and instantly became enraged? That moment continuously plays in your head because you wish you had responded differently, right? Now all of a sudden you are angry all over again. You have just caused yourself stress, anxiety, and potentially depression because you haven't released the anger bottled inside you. Now you feel nauseated and sick because you have withheld the anger and frustration instead of addressing it and releasing it.

So, ask yourself, is it worth jeopardizing your health? The answer to that is no because, over a period of time, these feelings will only lead to even more destructive health issues. Mentally you have to realize that you cannot yield those negative feelings because, ultimately, it's detrimental to yourself.

Humiliation in Forgiveness

Rather than allowing our egos to dictate the relationship we have with others, we need to willingly eliminate the behavior of unforgiveness. We often get stuck being okay with disregarding people. We are seemingly fine without having any dealings with that person. Yet, I've discovered that more often than not, deep down inside, we really, truly miss them. We quietly long for the opportunities to see them, we secretly yearn for their phone calls, and we even feel anxious when someone mentions their name.

Oftentimes, the other party is ready to move forward with an apology or to have a hard conversation as to why something happened, but still, we reject them. We allow ourselves to reject the possibility of moving forward because we have become comfortable with the normalcy of unforgiveness. We allow pride to dictate how we move forward, despite the fact that deep down inside, we are suffering.

Reflect: Think about a time when someone wanted to apologize to you and you rejected them. What would you need to hear from that person to accept the apology and move forward?

_____

_____

_____

_____

_____

_____

_____

_____

_____

_____

_____

_____

_____

_____

_____

_____

_____

_____

_____

_____

Humiliation in Unforgiveness

Reflecting on how I felt when my grandmother and estranged friend passed publicly, I was embarrassed. Some knew of the broken relationships I had with both of them. Some knew that our relationship had not been repaired. However, it didn't mean I no longer loved them because, in all honesty, I did. However, my pride and my fear of potentially being hurt again in some capacity would not allow me to move forward while they were on this earth. I knew that things would never be the same. It is very difficult to forgive someone I loved when I had trusted them with my heart. Therefore, going forward, I guarded my heart for the possibility of being hurt again.

Coming face to face with the people they were close to in the days following their deaths made me feel ashamed. Ashamed because I was now grieving for someone with whom I no longer had a relationship. It's not that anyone, in particular, made me feel ashamed; it was all me. Internally, my guilt was terrorizing my mind. I was sure that everyone around me was aware of the opportunities I missed because I was unwilling to get things right. I chose to be difficult all the way up until their untimely deaths. In their deaths, I was hurting and extremely devastated. My heart was shattered. I wanted to grieve, but in no way did I want anyone to think I was playing the victim in their death.

We often think we have time to make things right. We assume that at some point, when we are ready, we can potentially reconnect. "Having time" is the most selfish ideology we have. The time I thought I once had, expired. So publicly, I did my best to shy away from expressing my emotions. It troubled me how others would view me for grieving. I often wondered if I even had the right to grieve. Feeling defenseless in the eyes of the public, I bottled those emotions. Once I was home, or amongst people I was closer to, I completely lost it. My emotions were uncontrollable. I had to accept the fact that there were no do-overs. That was one of the most troublesome feelings I have ever had. Thankfully, through prayers, conversations, and support, I eventually found peace.

Guilt and Grief

Guilt and humiliation really go hand in hand. When I lost my two loved ones, I knew I could have done more to iron out our relationship. Unfortunately, I didn't think or even consider it then because, as the old folks would say, I was stuck in my ways. Immediately after their passing, I ruminated on how I could have confronted the concerning issues to find some type of resolution. I had to accept the fact that there were no do-overs. Knowingly, I had rejected the possibilities of reunifying. Sadly, I had waited too long.

Reflect: Have you ever lost someone unexpectedly and didn't get to resolve any issues

you may have had? What would you say to them if you could?

_____

_____

_____

_____

_____

_____

_____

_____

_____

_____

_____

_____

_____

_____

_____

_____

_____

_____

_____

_____

_____

_____

Battling Self-Accountability with Forgiveness

My lack of trust restricted my heart and mind from any possibility of reconciliation. However, once you accept that you can't change what has happened, you need to determine if you can move forward or not. When I reflected on the causes of our deteriorated relationships, I should have fixed things. I should have been more open to listening, understanding, and being more compassionate about their feelings. In hindsight, I caused myself even more pain by not addressing my concerns. I dismissed chances for reconciliation even when the olive branch had been extended my way. Oftentimes, the person who feels victimized holds on to everything, is irrational in their thinking, and is quick to point out the fault in others. We have to take accountability for the role we play in an alienated relationship. Remember, too, once you accept your role, you must forgive yourself. It frees you from any guilt you have suppressed within.

Think about your behavior when you're consumed with unforgiveness. Oftentimes, the effects of unforgiveness left me extremely moody and depressed. Oftentimes, it kept me from having a relationship with my children. So, not only was I suffering, the children were suffering as well. Sadly, they were unaware of the rationale behind my actions. Emotionally this habitual offense can begin to cause a strain in your other relationships. This is why it is imperative to forgive because it detaches you from depression, anxiety, and a grudge-filled heart. Most importantly, you want to rid yourself of the possibilities of resentment that could develop in your children or any loved ones due to your actions. As parents, we have to be cognizant of our behavior because the error of our ways becomes the habits of our babies.

Learning Along the Road to Forgiveness

My own journey of forgiveness has taught me how freeing, forgiving others and yourself can truly be. Your whole being will become liberated from the hurt and pain you have had bottled in from the wrongdoing of another person. Don't be mistaken, forgiving what has happened can be extremely difficult. The actions are not excusable or forgettable. Most often, it's very hard to forget what has taken place. Your feelings are yours, and no one can tell you differently.

Forgiving someone who has hurt you does not negate the fact that the action took place. Frequently, the person who hurt you assumes that once they've received forgiveness, everything will return to normal. More often than not, that doesn't happen. Once a person has wronged you, it can be really unsettling to be around them. On my journey, I have become a huge advocate of peace. If it doesn't bring you peace then you should remove it from your life. Most people assume that you have to be around a person to forgive them. This is not true. Remember, forgiveness is necessary for your healing. Once you have clarity and take accountability for your actions, you can forgive and move on. It is okay to remove yourself because some people are not good for you. Some people have ill will and cruel intentions. You must recognize those signs. That is why it is beneficial to acknowledge your spirit of discernment. You will be able to identify behaviors that are not suitable for who you are and who you are becoming.

* * *

Reflect: What is the longest period of time you have stayed upset with someone? Was it that detrimental that you couldn't let it go?

_____

_____

_____

_____

_____

_____

_____

_____

_____

_____

_____

_____

_____

_____

_____

_____

_____

_____

_____

_____

_____

_____

Forgiveness Now vs. Forgiveness Then

It is amazing how you go throughout life continuously learning how to make better decisions for yourself. Not realizing that the simple things we've been procrastinating on correcting are the exact same things that are causing us the most harm internally. Taking care of your mental, emotional, and spiritual needs is an ongoing practice. That's why it is important to continue to grow, nurture and cultivate your sense of self. Being honest with yourself is a huge component of this growth. This is why it is imperative to love yourself. Acknowledging how dope you are and realizing how important peace of mind is, is not only a lifesaver but a game-changer as well. Things that are set out to disrupt your inner calm will no longer bother you.

Now, we are only human, so there will be instances where situations will bother you. In those cases, talk through them. Explain how the words that were said or the actions that took place bothered you. The worst thing that we do, or that I have done is to allow the situation to fester. The more you allow the incident to sit without addressing your feelings, the angrier you will become. That is why it becomes so much more difficult to forgive and move on. Identify the cause, discuss it with the other party, and let it go. Hopefully, they will own their wrongdoing and apologize. Or, they may not. Unfortunately, getting a genuine apology from someone is not always the case. You may never receive an apology. However, you will get to the point where that is fine. At that point, accept what it is and move forward. The release is therapeutic, and your heart will become so much lighter. You do not need their apology to move on with your life.

Once you grasp the importance of self-love, you will begin to demand the same from others. As we continue to learn, our actions will reflect that. You will be more open to acknowledging your faults. `You will make more rational decisions and, in return, receive more positive results.

Reflect: How has an unforgiving heart affected you emotionally?

_____
_____
_____
_____
_____
_____
_____
_____
_____
_____
_____
_____
_____
_____
_____
_____
_____
_____
_____
_____
_____

The End is Just the Beginning

FORGIVE! If it's not affecting your health, wealth, or family, let that hurt go. Once people with whom you have unresolved issues transition from this life, you are left here on earth with regret. We have to stop putting things off like tomorrow is guaranteed. We should not be so naive as to believe we have more time. The aforementioned has been a true testament that life does not wait on us. Once you consider how an incident affected you, look deep within and evaluate how you can move forward. A lot of the negative situations that we experience and bottle up inside need to be released. Release these feelings now to move forward without dwelling on something so minuscule that it ultimately causes more heartache and pain. It is worth more to talk through what has hurt you than to allow it to fester over time, causing mental instability. Life is so much better when you are no longer holding onto disappointments.

Acknowledgments

The love and ongoing forgiveness of our Lord and Savior have helped me through everything and especially the toughest times of my life. Where would I be without my devoted family and loyal friends? Life has not always been easy, but I'll be remiss if I didn't acknowledge my incredible tribe and blessings. Through everything I've endured, my daddy has been there. Thank you, daddy! Thank you, Step for being supportive. I also want to recognize my loyal and dedicated friends, Tenika, Christa, Tamika, Martina, Nisha, Erica, Kim G., Katrina, Tijuana, Aurelia, Leslie (4ever4life), Keila, Tara, Catrina Price-Simpson (RIP), La'Porchia, and Neka. Nikki White, I remember all the convos and scriptures you would recite to me while growing up regarding forgiveness. You have always encouraged me to have a forgiving heart. I wish I had listened earlier.

Dominique G. and Neanna, thank you for giving me the closure I needed to move forward. Your words and thoughtfulness help alleviate the guilt I carried so heavily within. These friends have different timelines within my life, but they all play an intricate part in me evolving to be better than the day before. They have been there during the happiest times of my life and the most devastating times of my life. There has never been judgement, and they have always listened with an open heart and mind. I'm forever and grateful.

To my siblings that are there no matter what; Bianca, Ombreyam, Everett, Jasmine, Justin, and Melvinie. You ever have a rider who is there no matter what? I must acknowledge KC for always being there and offering a shoulder to cry on during some of the most difficult times of my life. Marquita Shanita, thank you for being the best graphic designer and for everything you've done for 4ever4life. Tanya, thank you for always listening and being a voice of reasoning. I'm sure mommy is happy you're looking after me and your cousin/grandbabies. I'm grateful to each of you! Thank you for contributing to my growth.

Aurelia

Who Am I.....

Virginia Native, I am a Daughter Sister, Auntie,
Cousin, and Friend with a connection to many GOD
has placed and will continue to place along my
life's journey.
The Unicorn- Chosen, different, special, rare, one of
a kind, misunderstood, abandoned, and unfamiliar.
All these words have been used by many to describe
me. If you have ever heard any of these words being
used to describe you just know this.....

Anything different, and rare is valuable!

Dedication

I dedicate this book to those GOD has placed along my life's path. If you are reading this dedication, you have been added to walk along my life's path. We are all connected through HIS plan and purpose for our lives. Thankful for the lessons, love, and growth along this journey. I pray this book, connections, and encounters with me have brought something to your life, just as you have/will mine. We are truly connected for a reason, season, lesson, purpose, and/or a lifetime. One Love 4EVER 4LIFE.

The Unicorn

We all have a life story that has the good, the bad, and sometimes the ugly. I have started, stopped, completed, and closed many chapters in this life. However, through it all, my story is still being written as my life continues to evolve. Do not allow life's adversities to define, hinder, and stop you at your current chapter. Continue the journey to write the ending as it is to be. Life is designed and planned to get us to our true purpose and destiny. Even with God taking the lead, there may be the good, the bad, and sometimes the ugly. Remember, His purpose is always greater than ours. This is the greatest part of life; if we are blessed to see another day, it's another chance to start, stop, rewrite, complete, and/or close the chapter we are on through God's direction, guidance, and grace.

It's not through the connections we choose to make from our free will. It's through the divine connections that God makes when we allow the pages of our story to be written that are planned, purposed, and destined. This has become my learning in allowing God to lead me as my differences are revealed to become The Unicorn into my 4ever4life journey.

You Have a Purpose

"For I know the plans I have for you," declares the Lord, "plans to prosper you and not to harm you, plans to give you hope and a future" (Jeremiah 29:11).

Unicorn- Chosen, different, special, rare, one of a kind, misunderstood, abandoned, and unfamiliar. All these words have been used by many to describe me. If you have ever heard any of these words being used to describe you, just know this...

Anything different and rare is valuable!

My Journey to an Awakening

Men.

As I sit to write this, I realize that so very often, I thought my life was about the men I brought into my life. I placed above all things and endured all that I did behind men and my free will of choice. I was seeking ways to cover my feeling of being different to experiencing acceptance. The answer for me became a man. As I think back over time, I have always felt and known that I was different; I just never truly understood how to embrace it. Along this journey, once I started to listen and pay attention to that small, still voice that I'd heard but ignored for so long and started being obedient to what I heard from God, I learned my journey was not about the men, but it was about ME and what God had planned and purposed for my life. The men, and my differences, are just a part of the journey and the testimony that I will share with you today.

As I started listening, being still, and obedient, I discovered that my life was already ordained to be much different than I thought. While I was busy looking at my life from a human aspect, God was busy preparing me to experience my life from a spiritual aspect, to be of the world and not in the world (see Romans 12:2).

Today I share my journey from my place of what I call the "Awakening," which started me on a course of self-discovery, self-love, and unconditional love. During this time, I learned about the importance of Godly connections that helped me in becoming the real me, "The Unicorn". Since childhood, I have always felt different. It was as if I did not fit in this world because there was no one quite like me. I tried to hide and cover this uniqueness by trying to fit in by being perfect and ensuring that I became who and what everyone wanted me to be.

This pattern and behavior became a part of my everyday life to fit in, to conform, to get along with, to do for, to keep the peace, and to take care of everyone. In my mind, hiding seemed like the right thing to do to take care of other's needs, wants, and happiness while discarding my own. I thought my purpose was to serve others, not fully understanding from a spiritual aspect what it meant to be a servant of others. It wasn't until much later on in life that I realized I was struggling because I was approaching life from the human aspect, not the spiritual. Thankfully, there were people in my life who were clearly able to see straight through my vulnerabilities, my fear of rejection, and my need to be perfect. This would set the course for many different life lessons for me.

You know the saying, "You just know what you know?" Those times when you have a feeling of knowing you are different but are not able to explain it in human words? Well, that was me. For as long I can remember, there were things that were happening to me that I just couldn't explain. I could see things, understand things, and often heard a strong, bold voice that provided guidance and insight. My peers picked up on this, which caused me to be teased, bullied, rejected, and isolated. In an attempt to be accepted, I pushed my differences aside and did what I thought I needed to do to be perfect. I worked hard to ensure that I became who and what everyone wanted me to be. I became a people pleaser, hiding my voice and myself away because I did not want to face rejection.

I start this story from the events that started me on the course of my First Awakening and continue on through many more events that have brought me to the life I have today. These experiences and life lessons started my journey of completion, and I am now writing this in the eighth month of 2020, a season that represents my New Beginnings.

My First Awakening started with the realization that my early life of being everything to everyone was slowly starting to unravel. The curtain was being pulled back, revealing all the things I had worked so hard to cover up to keep my true self hidden. Remember the men I mentioned I focused much of my life around? There are three significant ones that set me on the course to become the facade of a woman I was when I encountered the fourth who I thought would be my forever, my last, my end.

• • •

Reflect: Have you ever worn a mask? Pretended to be someone you were not? Put on a smiling face in spite of pain or sadness? How did it make you feel?

_____

_____

_____

_____

_____

_____

_____

_____

_____

_____

_____

_____

_____

_____

_____

_____

_____

_____

_____

Relationship Number One

I had convinced myself that if I could find a man to love me, all I had to do was keep everything hidden and be the person they said I should be. If I did that, I would be okay. I believed that I would finally be fully accepted, and I would never be faced with rejection again. The first one taught me so many lessons. He set me on the course of truly understanding the feeling of knowing what you know but cannot explain it in human words, which I had discovered early on as a child. My first encounter with him was seeing him across a crowded club. My eyes locked with his, and I had this immediate feeling of knowing I would love this man for life. He would go on to become my everything above all else.

Loving and watching him, I learned how to be a go-getter, to value money, status, and labels, to worry what others think, to hide my true feelings, to be emotionally unavailable, to be silent, to never quit, to hope, to dream, to believe, and to become who and what others wanted me to be. This was right up my alley. I needed someone who would teach me how to cover and hide because I was working so hard to hide the true me. Hiding behind him made it all so much easier.

Over the course of twenty-three years, I learned to master some of these things and others I failed at miserably. All of which caused me to overcompensate in other areas. Over the next twenty-three years, I followed, begged, and pleaded with this man to love me and to never leave or reject me because I loved him. I just knew that it was meant to be because I had that familiar feeling I had felt early on in life as a child of knowing what you know but cannot explain. From the start, I knew that this relationship was different and that this relationship was purposed.

Through all of the hard lessons, the leaving without a word, the cut-off, the silence, and the rejection, the one thing I didn't do was give up. I held on to the hope of the love I had for him. Although I encountered many losses, including the loss of my unborn twins that he denied were his, I loved him still; mind, body, and spirit. In all this, I gained two of the most valuable lessons that I still carry with me today. I learned forgiveness and the meaning of unconditional love.

Now through this on and off connection with Number One, over time, I learned all the things I told you from him so that go-getter in me, the status, and view of others were now the things I took from him and mastered. Number Two taught me about the heartache of infidelity and cheating. Although Number One was in and out of my life over twenty-three years, I never saw him with or caught him with anyone during my time with him. He would go on to have children, a life, etc., outside of me, but because he would ghost me, I never viewed his absence or rejection as infidelity/cheating. I know I told you I was different.

* * *

Relationship Number Two

My second relationship taught me that cheating and infidelity were a part of most relationships. I was taught to believe that no relationship was 'perfect,' and because of this, men would step outside of the relationship. It was normal, and as long as he came back, everything was okay. I didn't like the feeling of being cheated on in our relationship. I worked harder, did more, and tried to be more, all in the hopes that my efforts would make our relationship more perfect and keep him by my side. I believed that my imperfections were what led him to cheat. It simply made sense. I'd always been different after all, so, of course, he would look elsewhere. I felt like a failure.

Despite being miserable, I forgave him and allowed the cheating to continue. I took him back time and again. For years I tried to make it work, but because I felt that failing meant I wasn't perfect, I finally decided it was time to find the next man that could help me finally master my perfection. The lesson I walked away with from Number Two was that of acceptance. I accepted that it was over, and I moved on and found Number Three.

Relationship Number Three

Number Three got the collection of all I had learned and given to Numbers One and Two. I vowed to do everything in my power to make it work to take it to the next level of perfection. I gave 110% every day. I gave him everything I learned and gave to the previous two, but on an even deeper level. I poured myself into this relationship giving up money, time, self-esteem, material things, my entire self. If he asked, I did it at any cost, sacrificing all of me to be a perfect woman for this man.

I gave up every ounce of myself for this man. During our time together, all that had occurred in my previous relationships I endured again in this one, just for him to come to me one day and say, "You are too perfect; this cannot really be who you are. I know you will change if I fully commit to you, so I am moving on to someone who is more real and less perfect."

This revelation left me reeling. I was broken and utterly confused, but I was also determined. I walked out of this relationship vowing to prove that I was a lost asset. I vowed to remain true to myself and always to persevere. He rejected me for being 'too perfect,' and despite being down, I was certainly not out. The lesson I learned here was perseverance through life always, despite any challenges.

Relationship Number Four

This brings me to my forever, my last, my end. He would become 'The One.' I went into this relationship with the mindset to prove that I was real and that no matter what, I would not give up. I was determined to make it work regardless of anything that would or could come. This would be a forever marriage, with no possibility of divorce. I would persevere regardless of what life would bring me with this man. Little did I know he really would be my end. The true end of the perfect facade that I had created.

I set out on the course to finally be me, differences and all. Number Four showed me what it truly meant to be loved by another human being. I learned what it meant to be put first when needed, to give and take, to provide and to be provided for, to protect and to be protected. To have what I had always given to others now given freely back to me made our relationship easy to maneuver. I no longer had to work so hard to cover and hide who I was at my core. His love and care taught me to just be real, to be myself. He accepted me for me; the good, the bad, the ugly, the weird, the misunderstood, the different, and the spiritual.

Life was going along well. The lessons I shared earlier were all still embedded in me. Having all the attributes and learned behaviors, by this time, I was showing myself to be pretty good without much effort. I was able to share my dreams, my thoughts, my voice, my visions, my hopes, and most importantly, I shared God with him. We truly had created a world of love, wealth, status, giving, and spirituality. But having all the materialistic human things and living in the world would come with the costliest price of all my lessons. It would cost me, ME.

The discoveries that would come from what I thought would be my forever, my last, and my end were about addiction, mental and physical abuse, loss, mental illness, rebuilding myself, and finding my true purpose through New Beginnings. My forever, my last, and my end suffered at the hands of drug addiction. Drug addiction was nothing I was familiar with. I had heard of it but never really encountered it firsthand or knew anything about it. During this time, I reverted to what I knew best to do: stay, hide, pretend, cover, fight, and persevere. The daily mental abuse that started a few years into the marriage had now become physical. The physical abuse caused permanent physical damage to my body. Damage that I am reminded of daily. I can remember thinking back to movies I had watched depicting abuse and the numerous conversations I had regarding abuse over the years. My response was always, that could and would never be me. I would not be in that situation.

I flashed back to everything I'd learned in my previous relationships; the status, the go-getting, the keeping up appearances, the covering up, the persevering, and to stay the course always. So, I stayed through it all. In staying, I could prove to everyone, including myself, that I was not a failure. I could not allow anyone to see all of the parts of me I had hidden for so long. I couldn't let this façade of a life and of the woman I had created and presented to the world daily be revealed. Not one part of all the things she accepted, endured, had become, and hidden so well over the years could be exposed. If I let it be known, what would people think of me, how would I be viewed, and more importantly, would I now be rejected by everyone, not just the men that had been in my life?

Concerned with all of this, I stayed and suffered great losses mentally and physically. I suffered the loss of two unborn children, the loss of one of my fallopian tubes (lying in hospital for surgery, this man came to the hospital for money for drugs and left). To this day, I am unsure if the numerous beatings and other mental and physical damage suffered played any role in me having as many complications as I did while trying to become a mother. Along with making the decision to stay, adding insult to injury, because of his addiction, I/we lost all the material things.

The greatest loss that came from this was the loss of my spirituality. The same spirituality that I had finally embraced and that he openly accepted and allowed me to share. When we first got together, he was open to learning about God and even gave his life to Christ. His childhood upbringing had turned him away, but our relationship turned him back towards God. As time went on, however, between the drug abuse and his neglected mental illness, the spirituality and relationship with God that he had accepted, developed, and embraced was now being used against me. I was accused of cheating, loving God too much, and being fake about my beliefs and my gifts. You name it, he used it.

This daily tearing down truly had me questioning God. What was happening to my life? I began questioning who I was. What was my place, my purpose, and was all of this occurring because I was different? At this point, I just did not know who I really had become or what I was supposed to do next. For the first time in my life, I felt helpless and hopeless. After twelve years of marriage (seven years physical, five years on paper) and what felt like a lifetime of dealing with addiction, mental and physical abuse, thefts, arrest, and countless humiliations, I finally gave up on the marriage.

The one thing that remained with me during all of this was prayer. Even through all the confusion and questioning, prayer was always there. I truly and literally stood on God's word, and I prayed as I had never prayed before.

One night a feeling came over me, compelling me to pray for something I had not prayed for before. I was quietly reading, praying, and standing on God's word, and all at once,

I felt like I did when I was a child, the "knowing that I know" feeling. That night I got on the computer and started searching for Number One. By this time, it had been over seven years since we last communicated. The internet was becoming popular, so I stayed up searching for him for hours. I have to add that I had searched for him on and off over the years and at one point even had a Private Investigator trying to locate him but had no success.

After hours of searching, I was about to call it a night when I came across a MySpace page that he had not been on for over two years. I took my chances and sent a message to the outdated MySpace. I woke up a few hours later to a message reply. He shared that he had been looking for me as well, and he thought I was replying to a message he had sent just the day before to a Yahoo account that I never even received. What would be the odds and the timing? I share this story to say that on that night, I prayed a specific prayer and the actions and answers that transpired within hours completely restored my faith in God.

Little did I know that the reappearance of Number One in my life would bring on a heartache that I had never experienced before. This pain was like no other, even after all I had been through. This hurt would become one that would truly reach the depths of my soul that I didn't know existed.

Rediscovery

Although I experienced pain like no other from Number One, the one good thing to come out of it was it caused me to turn back to God with all of me. I discovered the person I had become and made myself to be was still a part of me and had some control over me, but only God could heal me and align me with the people and things I needed in my life. So, I began the work.

I never went back to questioning but instead learned how to talk with God how He had tried so often to do in years past where I ignored or brushed Him off. During this awakening, I learned to ask God questions and to seek guidance and direction. I asked God to guide me, order my steps, show me my purpose, and reveal the true me he had created me to be, with all of my differences, to make it plain and clear along my life path.

My relationship with God became like no other I had in the past with Him. When I increased my obedience, talking, prayer, and reading of God's word, my whole spiritual life started to change. God gave me back so much more and on a much stronger scale. The very love that I had fought so hard to hide from, get away from, and was afraid of due to fear of what others would think, was the very love that was saving me, growing me, accepting me for who I was created to be. I continued daily prayer, talks, reading, and standing on God's word, listening, journaling, and meditating. During this time, God gave me a very detailed vision, like he had done many times before in prior years, but this time I embraced it versus fighting it.

In 2013, God gave me the first detailed vision in some time. It was that I would move to Charlotte, NC. I shared it with a friend. I told her I did not know what it all meant, and I was a little reluctant because I couldn't see myself in the Charlotte area. For a while, even though I could see what God was showing me, I rode the fence on the vision. I spent the next year being in God and His presence. God had many conversations with me and showed me many different sides of Him and His glory through my meditation, journaling, hearing, and reading during this period. He was showing and speaking to me about my differences, telling me that there was a greater purpose for me that was beyond myself and my own understanding.

I finally gave up the marriage that was, at this point, only on paper. Years passed, during this period I was still trusting in God, never fully understanding I had more losses to come. I was going through the loss of a marriage that I thought would be till death. I lost much more than that. At this point, all I had left was my job and my home. I poured all of what was left of me into my job, which was in teaching and facilitation. I must share that I was never one who could speak in front of others. But God spoke so clearly to me that this would all be preparation for what was to come. As I often did, I heard but ignored. I was at the point where I had lost full control of the life that I thought I was controlling so well. The curtain was pulled back, and every aspect of my life was revealed. The façade of the life I created and the person I portrayed was exposed. I can laugh today because the knowledge I gained is that I control nothing, and that has become a part of me that is still a daily work in progress.

Reflect: Could the setbacks you've encountered really be preparation for something to come? Have you ever experienced something so difficult you thought you wouldn't make it through, but because of God, you did and are now better for it? How have the experiences of your life shaped your relationship with God and others?

_____

_____

_____

_____

_____

_____

_____

_____

_____

_____

_____

_____

_____

_____

_____

_____

Divine Connections

The job that I poured myself into would present the next period of awakening and present a true lesson in divine connections. At the time, I was very much living in the physical and pretty much gone mentally. When my job sent me to Virginia to train, I made a divine connection- "Courtney," who you met as, The Professional, in this book. Upon meeting, the first thought I had was that she was much younger than me, and because of the age difference, we probably would not have anything in common. However, there was an instant connection. It was another one of those moments when you know what you know but cannot explain in human words. We just connected. We sat and talked about what seemed like everything under the sun. I left that encounter thinking how wrong I was to have judged her because I could see we had a genuine connection.

By this time, my life was in complete shambles. All I had was my job, but now I had uncovered this connection with her which I would later learn was only the first of several divine connections to be made. Over the next few months, we talked almost every day. We devised ways to teach classes together and often found ourselves in the same place at the same time. We formed a very special bond. During our many conversations, she accepted me for just being me. I did not have to hide who I was. All of this was during the period of God working on me, showing me my spiritual awakenings in Him. He was continuing to heighten and strengthen my spiritual gifts. The connection that He created allowed me to share these visions, talks, and awakenings with her. She accepted and embraced me as I was. She accepted all the differences that had always been looked down upon and rejected. Here was someone other than God accepting me for me. She understood who I was becoming as I was learning to accept and embrace myself. As the months passed and our connection grew, the next loss I was to endure, happened.

After nineteen years and eight months, the one thing that had kept me going, my job, was eliminated. The one good thing in my life, besides the connection I had created with Courtney, was gone without warning. January 29, 2015, was the day that my life was forever changed, and I will always remember the date because it was also my mother's birthday. Remember I talked about the importance of connections? Well, this day showed me that many other connections would come in my life that will never allow me to forget God's divine plan and purpose for my life as long as I listen and am obedient to His word and will.

I remember sitting in the office with the Human Resource manager as she talked about the elimination of my job. I could tell she was in shock. She apologized over and over and showed true genuine compassion for the situation. To this day, I still cannot explain or describe it in human words but I had a peace beyond understanding. But God! All I can translate it to is BUT GOD! Despite the loss I experienced, it was me who comforted the visibly shaken HR manager. I just remember telling her it was going to be ok and I apologized to her that they made her deliver the news to me. I stood up and hugged her. When her eyes filled with tears, I once again reassured her it would all be okay because my faith was in God, and I knew that He has a plan and purpose. I shared my favorite scripture, Jeremiah 29:11, with her. At that moment, she told me that she knew I would be okay. I walked out of the office praying, and to this day, I've never shed a tear for this loss like I had shed so many for all the others. At that moment, I knew something had changed in me, and it was nothing BUT GOD that would keep me.

I went home and started to pray and meditate. I talked to God and told Him I trusted Him wholeheartedly. I knew He would direct my path - Lord, your will be done. For so long, I had tried my own will and suffered. It was now time to really hear, pay attention, listen, and not ride the fence on anything being spoken by God, no matter how off or crazy it seemed or sounded. I just had to truly trust at this point in my life because there was nothing left. I had lost everything but the roof over my head.

● ● ●

The job gave us ninety days to find a new position if we wanted to stay on. I prayed and asked for guidance on what to do next. There went the 'self' part of me trying to decide what to do after I had prayed to God for His will. My human mind was thinking, do I really give up after almost twenty years? I decided I would just find and take any job I could, to just keep my time.

While all of this was going on, my coworker Courtney was called daily to check in on me. She was devastated for me, but I was at a place of inner peace, and I found myself comforting those around me. No one could understand my lack of worry, my calmness, and my peace. On that day, January 29, 2015, God changed me in an instant, and, in time, He revealed the next path I was to take.

A week later, I found myself back in 'self' mode again. I was searching for jobs, reaching out to my networks, and applying for pretty much any job I saw. When I realized what I was doing, I stopped and prayed, "God, if this is not your will, please show me." Immediately, God answered. My phone rang. On the other end of the line were my two younger sisters, who called to tell me that my middle younger sister (there are four of us: one older sister, then me, then my two younger sisters) was diagnosed with breast cancer. They told me that she needed to have chemo, and even though she wasn't sure what it would all entail, she was going to fight. During this time, my baby sister's mom was already going through chemo, fighting her own breast cancer diagnosis.

Then and there, I knew what I was going to do. God told me, and I decided I was not going back to work and not looking for another job; I was coming to help take care of her and be there for her. God spoke so; clearly, I just knew that my job had to end so I would be free to go be with her. I sat there in awe and said, "Ok, God, I hear you. I am going, I am listening, I am going to be obedient." I heard the Shekinah Glory Ministry song "Yes" and, "Your Will," by Darius Brooks at the height of my first losses and the many more that were to come. These were two of the very songs that got me through before. I listened and followed God. I was in full trust, a place I could not really recall ever being in before without having some misplaced reliance on myself mixed in.

It took a few weeks to get everything in order, but I packed a bag and moved to, of all places, South Carolina in order to be with my sister. I was a mere thirty miles outside of Charlotte, NC, the very place God had told me I would end up years prior. Making this leap of faith, coming to be with my younger sisters, we were able to build a greater deeper bond now that we were older and could truly grow to appreciate and understand it. I spent the next year learning and building deeply meaningful bonds with my sisters.

* * *

My younger baby sister and I had a prior bond due to her growing up on and off with my older sister and me over the years. However, this time we built a different type of bond than the one prior. My middle younger sister and I created a bond we had never had before due to the distance and growing up in different households. We both realized we were so much alike, had so much in common, and really missed out on a lot over the years.

After being in South Carolina on and off for a full year, I decided to permanently move to South Carolina, the very place I said I would never find myself being other than to visit. So, it was set. I moved right on the outside of Charlotte, NC. I just remember saying to God, "Ok, I am still trusting." After the move, my baby sister lost her mother to breast cancer. This period just solidified that I was right where I was supposed to be at the time I was supposed to be there and that God's vision had a purpose.

During this time, I continued to stay connected to my first divine connection with my prior coworker Courtney. She became an even more connected part of my family with my parents, an older sister in Virginia, and my sisters who lived in South Carolina. She moved from Atlanta, GA to Columbia, SC, then to, of all places, Charlotte, NC, because she took another role within the company that had eliminated my job. That divine connection made years earlier was still alive and growing.

● ● ●

While God was bringing all these divine connections into my life, my younger middle sister passed from breast cancer. While she might have lost the battle with breast cancer, ultimately, she won the fight because now, she was home with God. She had fulfilled her purpose here on earth and had gained her angel wings. Now in my life of what had become my New Beginnings, I suffered two additional losses of two women I had grown to love and who had become significant parts of my life during my New Beginnings.

A few months before my sister passed, I decided to go back to work after being blessed to be off for about a year and a half to have this time with her and my baby sister's mom. I decided to apply back to the very company that had eliminated my job years prior. The position and location that I applied to was the same location Courtney was now working at in Charlotte, NC. I got called for the interview. I did not share with Courtney that I had even applied until the day of my actual interview.

When I say planned and purposed...

First, I went through the interview with the Manager who was head of the facility, which I was later told was not normal protocol. Then Courtney and I met up for dinner after my interview to discuss how everything went. As we sat at dinner, the same facility manager with whom I interviewed walked in. What were the odds? Courtney and I were both in awe but knew it was another one of those "when you know what you know" feelings that we were experiencing together. Unicorn behavior!

Although I didn't get that job, because of my experience, I was offered a different role. I had applied for just an everyday role as I did not want the same type of responsibility I had prior. But when God has something different for you than what you have for yourself, He will work miracles. The HR manager from the facility called to go over the offer packet. Remember the HR Manager who had left prior to my job being eliminated, which caused the other HR manager to give me the news? He was the very one calling to go over my offer packet in Charlotte, NC, who had been my HR manager in Virginia. All a part of the divine connections. When I arrived, Courtney told me all about her role in facilitation. She talked about her coworkers and how I needed to meet them, and she could not wait to introduce me to them when I started.

Reflect: Have you ever received some startling news that rocked your world? How did it make you feel? How did you respond? What was the outcome? Was God in the mix of it all?

_____

_____

_____

_____

_____

_____

_____

_____

_____

_____

_____

_____

_____

_____

_____

_____

_____

_____

The Encounters

The first week on the job was full of daily supervisor meetings. On day two during the supervisor meeting, a lady stood up dressed in a pink Ralph Lauren polo with a pink sweater tied around her shoulders. She was speaking about dress code, professionalism, etc. I can just remember hoping to myself that I was not on her team and that our paths would not cross. There was nothing wrong with what she was saying, it was just that the presentation was given in a very blunt and matter-of-fact tone as if she felt she should not have to be saying all this and that it all should be a given. Well, again as the saying goes, do not judge a book by its cover, as I had done previously with my coworker Courtney.

I would be proven wrong once again and that when there is a divine connection to be made, God will do His work. My path crossed once again with the pink polo lady. She was on Courtney's team. The introduction was brief, and all I remembered was my first encounter with her. I knew that I would steer clear.

As time went on, I was introduced to Tijuana. Just a quick introduction, but I noted that she was kind of stand-offish and very pregnant. I recall, weeks later, I ran into her at the elevator. I spoke to her, and her greeting seemed very forced. I remember thinking, "Eewww, ok then."

Months passed and there would be occasional, brief encounters with "Jessica" (the pink polo lady) and Tijuana, which truly were all due to the connection we all had with Courtney. Not long after that, Tijuana was out on maternity leave. While Tijuana was out on maternity leave, Courtney, Jessica, and I met up every Friday after work for happy hour with another coworker. Before I knew it, Jessica along with the other ladies became a daily part of my life. The very woman I had hoped my path would not cross had become a fast and important friend. She was my next divine connection, another one that fully accepted me, my differences, and allowed me just to be me.

Time rolled by and Tijuana returned from maternity leave. I saw Courtney and Jessica daily, which caused me to encounter and reconnect with Tijuana a little more frequently too. This allowed us to create a different type of relationship. The 'hellos' we shared felt a lot less forced. We talked about going to the *2017 Essence Festival* in New Orleans, Louisiana (NOLA) together. We all agree to go - Courtney, Jessica, Tijuana, and I. This trip was what truly solidified and bonded our friendship on a level that proved it was a divine connection. We decided to drive to NOLA from Charlotte, NC, a 10-hour trip. When I say, it was no one BUT GOD that drove and guided that SUV and led the conversations for the ten hours because it truly felt like it was only about a five-hour drive.

• • •

Along the way, Courtney and I were asked why I call her Courtney and not by her actual name, Leslie. I shared the story of when she visited Virginia with me, and my mom kept calling her Courtney. My mom is one who cannot remember people's names. She was calling her Courtney with true conviction like that was really her name, and Leslie even began answering to Courtney. The inside family joke was born, and now Leslie is my Courtney. During the ten-hour drive, we talked, laughed, and shared so much. The four-day trip was great, and we decided this would become a yearly girls' trip, our newly created tradition. Little did we know that the movie *Girls Trip* was in the making and would come out the following year, significantly changing the Essence Festival's cost and accessibility.

During the course of that year, I was introduced to Cody. I often went up and visited Jessica, who was now in a new role, and Cody was a part of her new team. During my visits, I saw Cody, and while we spoke to one another, we did not have many in-depth conversations. Cody was loud, always laughing, talked a lot of trash, and took nothing from no one, so I made sure I stood my distance because her style was far above any I had encountered.

In 2018 we discussed taking another NOLA girls trip for Tijuana's birthday in December. Well, as I always enjoy doing, I found all the details for the trip, shared them with the group, and Tijuana and I booked our trip to later find out that everyone else had backed out of going on the trip. So, it was set. Tijuana and I would be the only ones going to NOLA in December of 2018.

I remember asking myself if just the two of us going on this trip was a good idea. The thought crossed my mind that I really didn't know her like that. All of our prior interactions had been group outings and this would be one on one and I would have to share a room with a person I really didn't know on that level. I considered backing out and taking a loss on the trip. I prayed about it and God said, go. When I heard his voice, I just said okay, planned to make the best of it, and immediately asked God to be the center of the trip for us during the time we were there. I'm glad I did because this trip was covered from the planning to the end of it in ways beyond anything I could have imagined.

The trip to NOLA with Tijuana was truly another one of those life-changing moments that I cannot imagine having missed out on. God keeps me in awe. Tijuana and I met up to go to the airport and said a prayer for a blessed trip. We arrived at the airport to see that our seats were not together and we were told that they could not be changed due to the type of tickets we purchased. We went to the gate, said another prayer, and asked the gate attendant about changing our seats so we could be together. He explained that there were not any seats available to make the change.

While we were walking away, a gentleman asked the same attendant to have his seat switched because he was separated from his family. He was also told it was not possible. As we all started to walk away, the attendant looked at our tickets again and said he could switch both of our sets of seats. The gentleman had a seat next to one of ours, and he had a seat next to the one we had. At that moment we said, "Look at God!" We both ended up with Premium seats. Smiling and thankful, we settled in our seats and began talking. We shared that we initially had reservations about taking the trip because we didn't know each other well, and then shared how we prayed about it, and God said, go (see Jeremiah 33:3). Both of us heard God say, go, which was confirmation that this was a planned and purposed trip.

Wheels up, off to NOLA we went. When we arrived, we ordered an Uber to take us to the hotel. Along the ride talking to the Uber driver about our trip and places to visit. The driver was speaking about God and His goodness and said we were going to have a blessed memorable trip. Another God confirmation. We could feel that we were in a blessed atmosphere from the people we encountered to just walking, talking, eating, praying, laughing, crying, and just enjoying being in the presence of God, listening to Him speaking to us in the city. I came to learn that

God truly had this trip planned and purposed so that we could see another level of Him, and of myself, that what I had always deemed different for, I once again was accepted for just being me. I was accepted by Him and by Tijuana, "The Preacher."

I discovered there was a call upon my life. I had kept so many things hidden, or I shied away from them, not wanting anyone to really know the depth of how I heard from and spoke with God. I knew that others could never understand. They laughed at me about it and discounted the things I would share. Here she was. God has given me a friend who could identify with and understand my hearings, my visions, and my spiritual gifts. During the trip, there was a moment where we went into immediate prayer as God was speaking to Tijuana. The trip brought about great experiences, conversations, miracles, and revelations of the trip and for things that have, would, are, and will come to pass. God gave me my spiritual soulmate, who was purposed by Him to do His will and His works. One message shared on this trip was God said that we would begin to see things we have never seen before. I have to say this trip was the best trip I had ever taken. The peace, joy, and understanding gained and given by God on this trip were feelings I will never forget. Since taking this trip, Tijuana and I have created a long-lasting bond of friendship unlike any I have ever had.

After returning from the trip, we talked almost daily. To this day, we often laugh at our connection and try to trace it back. All we really know is that our friendship was that of a divine connection from God with a greater purpose beyond us. Often when He is moving and/or speaking, one or the other already knows without having to say anything because He gives us the same/similar visions, messages, confirmations, conversations, and revelations. He truly has me in awe, continuous praise, and worship, unlike anything I have ever experienced before. The most beautiful thing that has come out of it has been the acceptance of me, my gifts, and a greater level in God with another awakening. BUT GOD is all I've got.

Going into 2019, we all spent time together and with our broader connected circle of friends from our job. These connections brought us all together for different sharing, learnings, discoveries, knowledge, experiences, and deeper connections with our broader group of friends. We all know divine connections purposed our relationships; otherwise, chances are limited that we would have connected.

I shared with my friends that I could hear God speaking so clearly, saying that 2019 would be our year to get everything out of our systems and that 2020 would be the year that we will see so much and would have to capture it all. I just had this feeling, as I had often in my earlier years, of feeling different that I often ignored and kept hidden. However, my connected circle had embraced me and accepted me as no others had before. Feeling confident and accepted amongst my circle, in February of 2019, I bought 2020 planners and journals for the circle and shared that we would need them to keep track of what was coming. The growth, the dreams, the visions, the revelations, and what we would each experience needed to be documented.

By this time, as I have shared previously, I knew Cody as being in a mutual circle. She was one who scared me by her mere presence. Remember that mistake of judging a book by the cover and first impressions? I was once again proven wrong and shown that God is in control of all things. I control nothing, although at times I think I do. However with Cody, during this time, the visions and messages God shared helped us develop a bond. I shared my dreams, visions, and messages with her, but she would get what we called 'scary.' However as time continued, she became more open to hearing, sharing, and understanding the messages. She was not judging, but she listened, heard, and embraced what I deemed were my differences. Now I visited Cody almost daily and she became "Cody Co," the name I now call her.

As 2019 began, several things occurred. Although we had shared and discussed that big things were coming, I do not think any of us could have imagined the things to come to the level and magnitude that they did. Even with some of the messages and visions God shared, we knew something was coming but never imagined to the level in which he would show Himself to us all for his plan and purpose.

In April 2019, the job that had brought us all together to build the bonds and create the divine connections announced they were eliminating several positions and sending them overseas. We all later came to understand the job was truly for this purpose to bring us together wherein another circumstance we probably would have not connected otherwise. BUT GOD! The elimination of jobs impacted everyone in my immediate circle and most of our broader circle as well. However, through this elimination, my position was saved. At this moment, I began to feel that feeling of difference creeping in how I had felt all my life. Even more so when it was determined that all impacted would be bused to an offsite location, and I was standing there with the broader group and said we should all go together, and Jessica looked at me and told me I was not going with them. My heart went out to all that would be impacted however, those old feelings surfaced at the thought of being different and that of another loss.

Everything and everyone that I had come to love, cherish, and more importantly, those who had accepted me for me with all my differences, were leaving and my life once again was forever changed. All of this happened during a period where we were all going and growing through life. Visions continued, and deeper bonds were created. You could feel a shifting in all of us that could not be explained in human words, but we just knew what we knew even though we did not know exactly if that makes sense.

As I had the thought of feeling different, I began praying to God that He had to fix this. All of this was going on right during the period in my life where I was finding myself, my voice, being me through him, his guidance, and the divine connections he had placed in my life. I remember as if it was yesterday, praying and talking to God to fix it because I could not suffer another loss right when He was bringing me into my light, my path, my circle, and my purpose. God spoke so clearly, saying that this was not the end, but it will end and that this was much greater than this job. The job was used to make the connections. I was in awe and shared this with Tijuana. He had shared the same exact revelations with her that He would keep us all. She was not worried. Watching her, she had the same peace I had experienced four years prior with my own elimination. So, I understood, but it did not stop me from trying to fix it. Over the next few weeks, God would show himself to us all in many ways.

God's presence was so heavy in that building that Tijuana and I often stepped outside to fully praise and worship Him. One day, Tijuana and I were telling God, "You cannot do this; you have to fix it." Immediately God said, do not tell me what I cannot do. I will show you who I am and what I can do. God's spirit came over me where I was in full praise in worship. I could not even make it back into the building. I was outside in front, and Tijuana left me there in full praise. When I say God showed himself that day like never before, Jessica joined me and there we were, two women, out front in full praise, not caring who or what was going on around us or watching. At that moment, we knew that God had everything covered. Total, complete, divine intervention and covering. Tijuana showed up again later and watched. All we could all do was laugh as we stood in complete awe of God.

A few days later I prayed about taking a trip. God confirmed it. I reached out to my Virginia circle of girls that I had known either my whole life and/or over 30 years. I went to the job with my North Carolina circle, and I did what I do best. I said I was planning a trip for the next month in May for my birthday to NOLA, one of my favorite places to visit. With all that was going on, we needed a getaway. Everyone agreed. We also agreed that no one could back out once we planned and booked the trip. Along the way leading up to the trip, there were a few behind-the-scenes hiccups but all I knew to do was pray. I let go and let God take control of the trip and who would be on it with me. I knew this was one I could not control, and I just let go because I know He told us to take the trip.

This was yet another purposeful trip. Ten of us planned to go, and after praying and letting God do His will- it ended up being eleven of us that went. Those that know me, know I have a connection to the number eleven (11:11) something that I noticed during my first awakening period after my grandmother's passing. Well, the eleven women that went were not the initial ten VA/NC circle I had planned to go with. When I let go and let God, He brought together eleven different women that had some direct connection to me and to the four spoken of in my story. It truly was a blessed trip of eleven women from all ages and different walks of life who came together to make a divine connection once again, all purposed by God.

Reflect: When is the last time you let God take control. Simply threw up your hands and said, "God, have your will!" then waited and listened? Are you afraid to give up that control? If so, why? How could trusting God fully improve your daily activities and quality of life?

_____

_____

_____

_____

_____

_____

_____

_____

_____

_____

_____

_____

_____

_____

_____

_____

_____

_____

The Miracle of Healing

After I returned from the trip, I continued to pray, worship, and speak to God, but on an even deeper level. God gave me another vision of things to come. God made it clear that this book would be a part of the things He has planned and purposed for His vision and glory. When I returned, I felt another awakening and knew that there would be more to come. I was having that feeling again, which was unlike the others I had experienced before. I couldn't explain it in human words. I shared some of the different things I was experiencing in dreams, visions, and messages, but some of the visions, and dreams were like no other. They were dark, and things were occurring physically but I brushed them off as coincidences or something that I had to have done to myself in my sleep.

Although I was seeing these things in dreams and visions, I could not understand why I was also experiencing them physically. In the later part of May, going into June, I woke up one morning from a dream/vision of being tortured. I felt like something was just majorly wrong. I felt a sickness come over me like nothing I had ever experienced. I recall praying and asking God to please not let me fall out in the bathroom, hit my head or something, and be found like that. I prayed for him to allow me to make it to just touch me to get myself together. I was able to make it into the kitchen to get water and to sit down long enough to gather myself. I got up, was able to get myself into the shower to get ready for work. As I was in the shower washing, I could feel something on my stomach that did not have pain or anything; it just felt off, not right. I got out of the shower to go look in my floor-length mirror to see what I was feeling. When I looked in the mirror, I could see what was like a wound/hole on/in my stomach; when I went to touch it, I discovered that my flesh was falling out in my hands.

At that moment, I did not panic and honestly, it never even entered my mind to go to the doctor. I just knew that God was who and what I needed. He was the only one that could fix it. Again, it was one of those moments when you know what you know but do not know how you know but cannot explain it in human terms. I got dressed, went to work, and talked to Tijuana as I did each morning. The day went on and Tijuana decided she was leaving early. So, she came down to my floor to let me know she was leaving. I told her I would come to her house when I got off.

This day I invited myself knowing what I had going on, God told me I had to share it with Tijuana, but I couldn't do it at the job. I got to her house. We talked about the job, God, life, etc., and I asked her if she believed that ghosts, spirits, and/or demons existed. She said she knew they existed but had never seen them for herself. I explained to her what I had been seeing in my dreams/visions, the torture and attacks I had been experiencing that I had shared I had been brushing off as coincidences or did to myself in my sleep. I told her that they had now gone to another level that I could not simply push away this time. I was unable to get out what had happened to me that morning. The words would not form. All I could do was show her the picture of the wound/hole. At that moment I was sure she was going to tell me to get out of her house. She looked and her eyes got wide, and she said, "Real (my nickname) this is above me, but I have someone I can call if you want me to." She said I replied in a small childlike voice and said yes, please call. NO ONE BUT GOD is all I had in my thoughts at the moment.

Tijuana made the call, but there was no answer. She called a few more times, but her calls still went unanswered. She told me that it was very unlike the lady she was calling to not answer or at least call her right back. After what seemed like a long time, the lady called back saying that she was out at the store and unable to talk. The only thing that Tijuana shared with her was that she had a situation that was above her. The woman on the line asked her to put me on the phone, and I told her that I had something going on from dreams/visions I have been having. She asked me if I would be at Tijuana's for a while. I said yes, and she told me that she would call back. We hung up and Tijuana and I waited. While we waited, Tijuana and I continued to talk. She gave me her book of prayers and her only bottle of holy oil. She explained that I need to read the prayers and anoint myself and my house with the oil.

By this time, it was around ten o'clock at night, and I had been at Tijuana's for a few hours. We talked a bit longer, but the call still had not come in, so I decided to leave to go home. Tijuana told me that if she calls back, she will just give her my number. I got home and immediately started to pray, anoint myself and the house with the oil, and began reading the book of prayers. After doing this, my phone rang. It was the lady from earlier, Ms. Mae. Keep in mind there had not been any discussion of what was going on other than I had been having dreams/visions. Before I could explain what was happening, she asked me two questions unrelated to what I had going on. Do you believe in God? Do you believe He can heal? I answered yes to both. Ms. Mae immediately started to speak and prophesy what was going on in my body. She listed everything I had discounted, from the cut across my foot, scar down my neck, to the knot on my head, all of which had occurred at different times over the course of some weeks. She called out that there was a sickness in my body, and there was an issue in my stomach area that needed to be healed. We prayed in the spirit for some time. She prayed over every inch of my body and prayed over my house. She could even see and describe parts of my house even though she had never visited it.

When she finished, it was well into the next morning, and Ms. Mae told me that it was June 1. 6+1=7 and we both said at the same time, "It is completed and all is done." We talked a little while longer. I prayed again alone and went to bed. I got up later that day around noonish. I said my prayers and got up to get in the shower. As I was in the shower, I was careful as I washed over the area of my stomach where the wound/hole was. I did not feel the wound/hole, so I got out of the shower, went to my floor-length mirror, thinking I was just missing the spot and when I looked in the mirror the wound/hole was gone. It was healed.

All I could do was just praise and thank God for healing me. I stood there in awe at what I was seeing or, rather, not seeing. I took a picture of my now healed stomach, sent it to Tijuana, and immediately called her. I was in full praise with tears, and could barely find the words to tell her it was all healed, so I sent her a picture on her phone. We were both on that phone full of the spirit in full praise and worship. I called Ms. Mae and when she answered, all I could do was just shout in praise while trying to explain to her that God had healed my wound/hole. I could not contain myself! After speaking with her, I called my mom in full tears and praise, trying to explain to her the ordeal I had been through, which scared her because nothing I was saying was audible. Finally, once I was able to get out all that had been going on and the healing that took place, we were both in full praise on the phone. Tijuana and I talked several times over the course of the day in full praise and worship, speaking of God's miracle and his grace.

That Sunday morning, Tijuana went to church and as she was sitting in the pew, Ms. Mae came up to her and asked to see the pictures. Tijuana was confused, but Ms. Mae insisted. "The pictures," she said, "I want to see the before and the after pictures." Mind you, I had never mentioned to her that I even took pictures.

Tijuana reluctantly pulled out her phone, and they both were in the church in full praise before service. Tijuana called me after church to say, "Real, you could have warned me that you told Ms. Mae about the pictures." All I could say to Tijuana was that I never mentioned the pictures. She was the only one I shared that with because I would not want anyone else to see that yet alone my stomach! We both laughed at what I said then were once again in full praise at the revelation that neither of us had mentioned the pictures. No one can tell me God is not real and is not a healer and a miracle worker.

Reflect: Have you ever experienced something you couldn't explain? Strange dreams or visions? Things that feel out of the ordinary? Maybe even supernatural? What happened? Who did you share it with? What was the outcome?

_____
_____
_____
_____
_____
_____
_____
_____
_____
_____
_____
_____
_____
_____
_____
_____
_____
_____

The Miracle of Life

Time passed, and July rolled around. We were all still going on with life knowing that many things were to be changing for many in our immediate and broader circles. The job eliminations were getting closer, first cuts were slated to happen in September and then again in October. My concern and the thought of the loss were still heavy on me even after all I had just been through. All I could focus on was my life changing and once again I had no control over what was to come. There was so much going on in my area that was remaining. We were nearing the full launch of a new program. There were some changes on the horizon that would dramatically change the dynamics of my team that I had worked so hard to build.

In a meeting I was told that my team would be taken away and that we would need to work with less which as it were we were already severely understaffed. We were told the experience was needed elsewhere. I asked a few questions about this change and based on the responses given, I was not pleased. I started to pray just to keep my shock and disappointment in check. I heard God say it's over, and in the end, all I could see was a vision of Him showing me all zeros and saying, "It's expired."

I got up to leave the meeting and said, "Ok, it's all fine, do what you will because I have God and I know he has me covered no matter what you all do or decide even if it's not right. God has me covered." I walked out, and my coworker, who is part of my broader circle and is like a brother to me, called out to me. I told him that I may not have a job come Monday after what I said, but I knew that God had me. My friend told me he had never seen me speak like that before. He told me I was not rude or anything, it was one-hundred percent on point and spoken so eloquently. I left work for the weekend not worried about what Monday would bring because I knew God had me covered. He told me so during the meeting.

After the miracle that I had just been healed from a month earlier, nothing could waver my faith. I told myself that the following weekend would be one of excitement, praise, and worship of God. The worries of the job would have to wait. Tijuana had been asked to be the guest preacher at a woman's day service at a local church. Another vision God had shared prior had just come to pass. Tijuana and I had been speaking about what God was doing and how he was moving. When the call came, we stayed in full praise and worship for weeks leading up to the service. We already knew because God had given the vision all we knew was that God was going to move all things and show himself once again into something and that we would see things we have never seen before. We knew the day of service was going to be a day of change and deliverance for two people because Tijuana had a vision earlier in the week and had that vision again that morning. I remember being filled with joy and excitement for the day.

I arrived at the church, walked in for the service, and I could feel the Holy Spirit so heavy in the sanctuary. It was such an overwhelming feeling of joy and peace much more than usual. As the service got started, I could feel the Spirit heavy on me because I began rocking. When I rock, my circle knows God is all over me. This was the first time I ever heard Tijuana preach. We had always had praise and worship all up in and through our divine friendship, but I had never heard her preach. Tijuana began to pray and minister to the congregation but it was not her voice I heard. It was totally different. It was not the voice of the person I spoke with daily. It was as if God was speaking through her.

The message was exactly what I needed to hear the word was for me. I had such a heightened sense of the Spirit and was filled with the Holy Ghost. The whole service was a blur. I just knew I was in the presence of God. There was an altar call and deliverance occurred that day. After service, I hugged Tijuana and in the midst, I heard a familiar voice that I had heard before. I asked Tijuana if that was...but before I could get it out, she told me that that voice belonged to Ms. Mae. I had never met her in person but all I could do was just hug her and thank God for the day.

All of us in the divine circle were in service that day, so we took pictures before leaving. It was Women's Day and we were all in white. White represents the Bride of Christ, surrender, harvest, light, righteousness, conquest, victory, blessedness, joy, Angels, saints, peace, completion, and triumph (see John 3:16, John 4:35). This day was filled with it all.

After taking pictures and finally ready to leave, Momma NC, Tijuana's mom, grabbed me by the hand and took me back to the sanctuary near the pew we were sitting in. Momma NC said to me, "*Reelyah* (her nickname for me) listen to what God is saying to you, let Him use you. Be obedient." I told her I would. Momma NC pulled me and said, "*Reelyah* do you hear me? Listen to God, let Him use you, be obedient." Again, I told her I would but she repeated it for a third time this time with a different tone that let me know that I needed to really hear what she was saying. I was listening. It was a while before I knew what this encounter really meant but God brought it back to my remembrance and gave me the full understanding.

We went to dinner after the service and spent most of the time talking about the service and the praise and worship that had taken place in God's presence. One of our friends who attended the service spoke about my praising and called me Shouting John. That immediately became the joke of the day. After dinner, my girls and I stayed back in the parking lot just talking and catching up. We were in full conversation. It was just something about this day that just had us all full and still high on God. We said our goodbyes, gave hugs and kisses, and we all just walked away thinking how thankful we all were to have each other and how we could not imagine life without one another.

<u>Surprise Encounters</u>

Remember the men I spoke of at the start of my story? Well, in their own time, one by one, they all reappeared. I ran into Number Two in a store. It was my second time seeing him in about five years. I ran into him and his wife about five years previously at my stepmom's funeral. At that time it had been eighteen years since I had seen him. He spoke to my family but did not say anything to me. So, upon seeing me in the store he approached me and spoke. We made small talk, exchanged numbers, and he shared that there were some things he needed to share with me. We continued talking over the phone and during the course of the week he told me that he lost his wife, was raising his daughter alone, and would love for me to meet her. He also shared that he had just prayed to God for a way to find me via Facebook or something. Talk about God!

I looked forward to meeting his daughter and we agreed to meet up that following Friday. One evening, I heard a knock on my door. To my surprise it was him! I was upset because I had never let him know where I lived. How had he found me? He told me he had an idea of where I lived, drove around the area, and simply looked for my car. Eventually, he found my car and my house. That should have been my first sign that something was not right but I brushed it off and we went to dinner.

That Saturday he had a funeral to attend but we agreed we would meet up at my house after church on Sunday. I stopped to pick up something to eat on the way home and we sat at my kitchen table eating and talking. After I finished eating, I instantly felt sick. My head started hurting but this hurt was like a pain I had never felt before. I tried to make it to the bathroom. I was vomiting and using the bathroom all at the same time. My first thought was food poisoning but my head was pounding, my ears were ringing and again this was a pain like no other. I just did not feel right and I knew this was bad. I was trying to get myself together. I was able to make it to my room and I remember sitting on the edge of the bed praying and asking God to please take the pain away.

Number Two was still in the house and he told me to just lay down and take an Excedrin. I told him I couldn't lay down, that I needed to go to the hospital and to call 911. He just kept insisting that I lay down. It was a fight to get him to get my phone to call 911. I just remember telling him if he didn't drive me or call 911 I was going to call the police and drive myself. I knew I could not wait for the ambulance and I literally lived two streets over from the hospital. There was so much back and forth about getting me to the hospital and I just could not understand why he would not just do it.

Deep in prayer, I heard God's voice once again but this time it was the clearest I had ever heard it before. He told me to get to the hospital and not to lay down. God said, "If you do everything that I tell you, I will save you. When you get to the hospital, they are going to ask you on a scale of 1 to 10 how bad your pain is. You need to tell them it's a twelve." I later learned the number twelve represents God's Power.

He also told me that I could not stay where I was in Lancaster, I had to get transported out. I finally convinced Number Two to drive me to the hospital. I got my phone, called my baby sister, and asked her to meet me at the hospital. I told her I was in a lot of pain, I didn't know what was wrong, and that I was going over to Lancaster Memorial. I also told her that I could not stay at this hospital and I would have to be moved.

I got to the hospital and I jumped out of my truck. When I went inside the hospital there was no one at the desk but the Emergency Room was packed with people. Finally, two ladies walked up and asked what the problem was. I told her all the things God told me to say. I said, "I have a pain in my head. It is the worst pain I have ever felt. I just need it to stop. You're going to ask me on a scale of 1-10 what my pain level is, and I'm telling you it's at a twelve." They took me back immediately to be seen. They were trying to get me on the table into an MRI machine but each time they went to lift me I could feel pain in my body and legs. I told them they had to stop. It was too much pain. I explained the pain was in the back of my head.

I remember being rolled back into a room. My sister was there having a conversation with Number Two asking what happened. He told her he did not know that I just complained about my head hurting. I was in so much pain. I asked them to please just stop the pain, so they gave me morphine. During this time I could hear Number Two telling my sister that he had to be at work so he needed to leave but he needed my house keys because he drove my truck over to the hospital and had left his truck keys in my house with all that was going on. She gave him the key and he said he would get his keys and leave mine. She thought nothing of it. By this time I started to feel the morphine kick in. Soon after, the doctor finally arrived. I can recall a Caucasian doctor in a white lab coat standing next to my bed. He told me that I was experiencing hemorrhaging on the brain and that they needed to transport me out to Charlotte Medical Center. At that moment I heard God say, "Let go now. Rest," and I passed out.

I was out for three full days. I was mostly unresponsive and when I could respond, I was incoherent. I was unable to recall the year, the president, my name. I was told I said it was 1945 and Andrew Jackson was the president. I would later learn that my sister had called Tijuana to tell her I was in the hospital on the morning I was transported to Charlotte but she could not go. They would only let the immediate family in. My sister said she would be on her way. Tijuana told me that she tried to wait for my sister to arrive, but could not. She got to the hospital and was allowed into my room. Once there she called the circle to let them know where I was and what had happened. Divine connections.

I woke up three days later to find that my family and friends were told that I would not likely make it due to the injury I had sustained. If I did, I would probably be unable to speak or walk, and if I did, I would not have the quality of life I had before the injury and would need around-the-clock care. Two aneurysms had burst on my brain and as a result I had suffered two strokes.

During the time I was sleeping, I talked and visited with God. He shared so many things with me. He spoke of the connections He purposed that we were all connected. He told me that we would have no lack, that we were about to see things that we have never seen before. He needed us to listen to Him because we all had a purpose to fulfill for Him. He told me that we must always be obedient to his word. I was told I shared these things and was laughed at. They thought I was out of my mind, but everyone told me that if this was the way they had to have me, they would take me as I was as long as I was still here. Tijuana journaled everything I spoke during this period. She knew what I was saying was real.

My momma, sisters, family, coworkers, Ms. Mae, Momma NC, my divine immediate circle, and my broader circle would visit me daily. Prayers were sent up. When my mom and sister arrived, my mom had decided that if I survived, I was moving back to Virginia, no question about it. I learned that my divine circle had conversations and discussions with my mom that they would take care of me because I could not go back to Virginia. They would figure it out and do what was needed to keep me in Charlotte, NC. They all knew I was meant to be in Charlotte, NC, because God had revealed it years earlier and he gave me the divine circle that he had purposed.

Waking up on the third day after being out, I did not realize immediately where I was but I saw my cell phone, and I remember picking it up, wondering why I had so many missed calls and texts from my team. I wondered why no one had answered them. I saw I had missed calls from my mom and sister. I called my mom's phone and she did not answer so I left a voicemail and proceeded to call my sister's phone. My mom answered my sister's phone, thinking someone was calling from my phone because at her last visit to me I was still unresponsive. She couldn't believe it was me on the other end. Once I finally convinced her it was, in fact, me, all I could hear was my mom on the other end praising, shouting, and thanking God. Little did I know it was a miracle that I was up calling, talking, and in my right mind. This is how my divine circle sees me and why they named me "The Unicorn." I am chosen, different, special, rare, one of a kind, misunderstood, abandoned, and unfamiliar.

• • •

Remember the men I spoke of at the start of my story? Well, they would all show back up during this time. When Tijuana, my sister, and I looked at my phone, we discovered that over the days that I was out and unresponsive, I had been having conversations with Number One which was seemingly impossible because I was not awake. We looked at each other in disbelief but knew that it was no one BUT GOD that could have allowed the conversations to happen. The context of the messages and conversation said all the truths that needed to be said that I had waited twenty-nine years to hear. Another miracle, shown.

Additionally, during this time, I received a messenger message from Number Three. I had not spoken to him in over fifteen years. I thought he was reaching out because he heard that I was sick in the hospital, but he said no he had no idea. He had wanted to reach out before but never did. That morning, God told him to reach out, so he did, and he just wanted to see how I was doing.

I gained many revelations about Number Two. After waking up, I learned that when my sister arrived at the hospital, he had my purse and went through it saying he was trying to find my medical card which was not the case because I had all of that when I walked into the emergency room and gave it to the lady at the desk. God had already prepped me on everything to do and say for when I got to the hospital to be seen. He apparently tried to take my cell phone but somehow left it behind, called it, and when my sister answered, he told her he could not remember where he put it, so he was calling it. When my mom and sister arrived to stay at my house, he had gotten my sister from Virginia's number from my baby sister because she said he kept calling my phone non-stop.

He called my sister in Virginia to see if she and my mom wanted to stay at my house and if so, to let him know, and he would go home. This fool had been staying at my house and acted as if he actually lived at my house. He still had my house keys from when he went back to 'pick up his car.' He had never left them on the table like he said he would. Instead, he had been staying at my house since the night he dropped me off at the hospital. He was even driving my truck and my car. When they arrived, my mom and sister told my circle that they did not know I had anyone living with me or that I was even dating but they did not want to put anyone out since they didn't know what was going on. They figured I hadn't said anything for a reason so they were going to get a hotel.

When I say my circle does not play, they went slam off. Tijuana set the record straight and explained to my mom and sister that he did not live with me and that I had just run into him a few days earlier. She continued by saying I had agreed to go to dinner with him and to meet his daughter but that he showed up out of nowhere at my house. She told them that I had gone out to dinner with him, just once, and that he should not have my keys or be in my house.

During this time, my dad even saw my truck pass by my house and called my sister, asking her why she was going the wrong way. That's when my sister explained that Number Two had my truck, had been living in my house without my permission, etc. My dad wanted to kill this man. Thankfully my sister was able to reason with him and managed to get him out of the house and get my truck returned.

I spent fifteen days in ICU only for protocol. It was unheard of that I had recovered without sustaining any injury. There were no lingering signs/indicators that I had two aneurysms burst and or two strokes. The rapid healing and recovery that my body displayed had the doctors and hospital staff in awe and disbelief. The only visible sign was the tube that was draining the blood from my brain. They told me that this was a first, and it was an absolute miracle.

The doctors determined that I would not need any type of occupational therapy, rehab, or any medication. Statistically, I should not be here today. My survival was truly my second miracle in two short months and all I got is BUT GOD!

Upon being released from the hospital, I stayed with my dad for a few days until my mom and sister could make it back down. When I returned to my house, I found that Number Two had pretty much raided my house, emptied out most of my bar, and taken things from my home. He had my trash service canceled and even had the trash can removed from the house. I later learned he even went to my neighbor's house after leaving the hospital to tell them what happened to me and asked them to pray. They shared he was almost in tears and everything. Such a performance, acting sincere and concerned.

This latest awakening lesson taught me that not all connections are divine. Sometimes connections are sometimes created by the enemy, but we try to make it what we want it to be or what the other person may want it to be due to our own choice of free will. These choices will allow the pages of our story to be written. The encounters with Numbers One, Two, and Three during this period gave me the one thing they had not done in years past. They apologized for the manner in which I was treated. s

Unbeknownst to them, and only by God's grace, they each gave me my release, my healing, my forgiveness, and the firm understanding that I did not need men to define me. All I needed was God. Because I am defined by who He has planned and purposed me to be in His image and His likeness. My faith, my walk, my belief in God is greater than it has ever been, and I will be forever grateful to Him for loving me as He does. I determined that I would be obedient to His Word and be very specific in my life and movements from that moment forward, allowing Him to order my steps.

Through this current journey and learning about divine connections, and getting to my divine circle shared in my story, I have come to see God's Divine Power, Purpose, and Plan. We all have become significant in each other's lives. We each have a bond with the other that may be different from the next. Each bond has connections purposed by God and designed by his plan without any issues, concerns, jealousy, strife, competition, or anything that could break these connections that have been bonded 4ever4life! I am truly blessed for my divine connections and circle. Never judge by your view, thoughts of the cover, or first impressions. If you do, you may miss out on the divine blessings and connection God has planned and purposed. I cannot imagine my life without any of them.

After reading my story, I pray that you will find something in it that you can relate to, that will touch you and/or allow you to walk away with what is purposed, needed for you. I pray that you may find a way to work towards your healing, your purpose, and your destiny. God has shared, "It's Time to Get R.E.A.L. (Release Every Affliction Live)," to walk into your purpose and destiny. There's more to come. It's already written and has been shown.

"The Pain That You've Been Feeling Can't Compare to The Joy That's Coming." Romans 8:18

<u>Acknowledgments</u>

I would like to give acknowledgment of this book first and foremost to my Parents, James Brown, John Addison, and my Mother Linda Johnson-Brown who has given, taught, and shown me nothing but support, learnings, lessons, wisdom, and unconditional love to prepare me for my life's journey.

To my grandmothers for living their life with strength, dedication, guidance, perseverance, and for raising their families in/with GOD, their values, and love. Mary V. Johnson and Mary E. Moore.

I would also like to give acknowledgment to my other birth divine connections, my sisters, Triege Addison, Natasha Brazzell, and Chanda Addison (continue to rest in God's arms until I see you again).

Acknowledgement to Donna Clark and Brooks Glover who have been my spiritual sisters, sounding boards, and ride or dies through it all for 27/32 years. No matter the time that passes y'all are always there.

I would also acknowledge my divine circle since birth and along my life's journey My Boo Boo Kitties (Charita Taylor, Lauren Haley, Angela Williams, Jada Howard, Triege Addison, and honorary Boo Boo, Kitty Kemberly Thornton).

• • •

Additional acknowledgment goes out to my family and friends that have always been there for me through it all.

I am just Tijuana.

Daughter of Lew and Carolyn. Great granddaughter of Sadie! Mother of four and grandmother. I have a B.A. from UNC at Charlotte and am a licensed Baptist Minister. But formality doesn't mean very much to me. What's most important for you to know about me is that I am God's chosen instrument. I am uniquely me. I am the PREACHER!! (Peace Reached Even After Complete Hell (with) Everything Restored). My assignment is to use my lifeline to demonstrate God's divine purpose and authority.

"Kingdom building requires all types of workers, especially those who specialize in brokenness, like me and you."

-TStraite

Dedication

To my Sisters in Christ,

As embarrassing and shameful as some of my life's situations have been, I must share my experiences. There have been many who have doubted that I would tell my testimony, tell my truths, because of the negative connotation attached. As Black folks, we are historically known for sweeping things under the rug. We have been taught not to address certain things, and to hold our heads high, pretending that they did not happen. Tell God and no one else. I myself have been reluctant to tell my story because of these reasons. I was embarrassed to say that certain things happened to me and that I allowed them.

Today, because of God's grace and direction, my vision is different. If I can help one person to feel not alone in what they are going through or have gone through, then I feel like my life's mission has been fulfilled. When I was going through my various storms, I felt that I had no one. I felt like I was all alone, with no one that I could possibly talk to who might understand. I want you to know that you are not alone. The truth of the matter is that I was not alone either. Unbeknownst to me, there was someone who was very familiar with what I was going through. I didn't know this to be true because they(whomever those were that had already overcome) refused to share. My goal is to start making strides toward correcting this behavior that threatens our culture. I will be transparent.

● ● ●

"They triumphed over him by the blood of the Lamb and by the word of their testimony, they did not love their lives so much as to shrink from death." Revelations 12:11

God knows and so do I. With God, all things are possible. You will survive. I know it does not feel that way or hasn't felt that way but trust God's process in you, even though you may not understand. The obstacles you have faced, the situations that you have had thrown at you, or the things that you have done personally do not negate your purpose in God. If God can use me, he can use anyone. Don't be shamed into believing that you are not called because of your past or even your present. God wants you just as you are. There is a purpose for all of us, "Damaged, Broken, Used and Misused," persons in the Kingdom. Kingdom building requires all types of workers, especially those who specialize in brokenness, like you and me. This is why God needs us; someone else needs our help to overcome their struggles. Get up, get cute, and let's go. We have a mission to accomplish.

Let's Get After It.

The Preacher

The forgiving heart of a Christian's nature does not qualify us as fools.

Complete fools, that is! We might have a lapse in judgment and/or a temporary delay in reaction, but we will eventually be able to see clearly. When we wake up, we wake up!

The awakening is on a whole other level. It's almost like a rebirth.

Excuse the double negative, but ~ I Done Woke Up. Been reborn again.

Right here is where I initially wanted to ask that you not stand in judgment as you read. But then I decided that I would not ask that because it is really okay to judge if you want. It really does not matter much to me anymore as I have been delivered from a people-pleasing personality. Personal experience has a way of changing one's perspective on judgment. Relax, and let's get after it! Free your mind if you can. I sure had to find that same freedom in order to start this mission of writing.

The people, the places, the things I have seen, done, and had done to me surely should have killed me, naturally and spiritually- but God. God preserved me for my purpose in Him.

I am the PREACHER (Peace Reached Even After Complete Hell (with) Everything Restored)!!

• • •

If you read the definition of a preacher, it is simply stated to be; one who preaches, especially a minister of religion. There are no prerequisites added to the definition. This speaks volumes to me because it confirms my qualification in Christ regardless of the fact that my character has not always promoted Christ.

"Father, if you are willing, take this cup from me; yet not my will, but yours be done." Luke 22:42

So many days and many, many nights I have asked God if he was sure that I was the chosen one, and/or could I please have permission to quit. I have tried to quit of my own accord more times than I can count. Even as I write, I am still waiting on God to say, "Nevermind, you don't have to do it." But I have come to the understanding that this is not going to happen. He has already told me what it is and how it is to be. My duty now is only to be willing, obey, and trust His process. I often reflect on just how damaged of an individual I was, how broken I was. I felt like man seemed unable to see my worth, which is why I questioned God's choice in selecting me. This is understandable because I didn't see my worth either. But I promised God that I would see this project through regardless of the distractions that come to discourage me.

I have disappointed God so many times that I owe him at least this act of obedience. I won't lie; I have been very resistant to embracing my purpose. I have even prepared myself for my own death, asking God to take me as I slept because the weight of the world was so heavy that I did not want to wake up even one more day. It's a grim place to be when you invite the peace that only death can bring. I have been so welcoming of death at times that I have actually enjoyed the planning of my final service, from the songs to be sung and the layout of the casket and flowers to the outfit, hair-do, and makeup. It is obvious that this specific prayer was not granted. Anyway, enough of the rambling.

Follow my path. Here we go.

Reflect: Can you relate to being in a grim place? Reflect on a time when you were in a grim place and how you moved past it. If you are in that grim place now, start jotting down a plan of action for change.

_____

_____

_____

_____

_____

_____

_____

_____

_____

_____

_____

_____

_____

_____

_____

_____

_____

_____

The Call

I want to first start by discussing the call on my life by God to preach and teach the Gospel. Like myself, you may have wondered what prompts one to accept "The Call"? Simply put, there was nowhere else to turn. Of course, having been a hell-raiser, a combative, slick-talking, sexually promiscuous chick from a single-parent home who had already borne two children out of wedlock, I definitely felt unworthy to talk to God, let alone speak for Him!!

I cannot tell you how many times I asked God if He was sure. Honestly, I still occasionally ask Him to confirm His need for me. By the time that I finally accepted the call, I had gotten married. I had been married for around four years when I finally surrendered. Notice I said by the time I finally accepted the call. You see, I had known that there was something different about me, spiritually, for a long time. I recognized with full understanding that I was spiritually gifted a few years earlier but still refused to say "Yes." I was running, running fast and hard. I guess running in place would be a great way to describe what was happening because I was getting nowhere in a hurry. I could not escape God's Will. I tried in the natural realm to turn off the spirit like you would a faucet. He kept speaking to me; He kept calling my name. He kept saving my life.

Speaking of saving my life, I have been in three major car accidents that should have killed me. The first one was around the age of two years old. I have been told that my mother and I had a collision with a tractor-trailer truck. The accident was brutal. My mother was badly injured in this accident. She was hospitalized for months afterward, even having to learn how to walk all over again. Still, today she suffers from some memory loss due to that accident. I walked away from it, unbothered, without a scar or injury. As it's told, I required no medical attention. I was found outside of the car that my mom was driving, indicating that I was thrown out. And get this—God even orchestrated it in such a way that I was found in the field by my own cousin who happened to be driving that way. She, my cousin, cannot explain why she took that particular route on that day. Notice I used the words "happened to", in the previous sentence, but of course, we know God leaves nothing to chance.

The result was the same for other accidents, I walked away, unbothered, without a scar. My oldest son, baby sister, and I were in a car accident in1995 where the car rolled over at least three times that I remember. When the car finally stopped tumbling, we were upside down on the outer bank of Highway I85. We all escaped the crushed car without any injury, not even a cut, as the Lord did not even allow the glass to break. Can you explain a crushed car with no broken glass? But God. **Crushing, shattering, and rolling over ~no scars. The**

protective and preserving presence of God. Nothing missing, nothing broken.

I tried to reason with God, telling him "not now". I need some more time to get my life in order. I kept on reminding him of who I was and what I had done in life, I reminded him of the years of sexual promiscuousness--looking for love in all the wrong places, looking for validation, degrading my temple just to feel wanted and desired. It definitely was not for pleasure, as there ended up being little to none of that. Yeap....I said it. Sin without satisfaction, and for what? Maybe there was no satisfaction because it was a sin.

The tug of war on the inside continued. I came to the realization that I had to have Christ as the head of my home. There was no other way it was going to work because I made no clue how to operate in a married, blended family home. As I started to seek a deeper relationship with Christ in order to understand and function as a wife and mother, my calling to ministry started to manifest itself. I could no longer deny God's hand on my life.

Marriage and the Call; I Do and I Do

On a Friday afternoon in March, we had a small, impromptu wedding with our closest family and friends. The very next month, I caught my husband cheating and confronted him.

I chuckle now inside as I recall that first incident of infidelity. But it was not funny at the time. I remember when I caught him on the phone with *her*. He was outside walking around the house, talking to her on the phone, and making plans for their next escapade. I overheard the entire conversation. Truth be told, at this point, I don't even know if he tried to be discreet or not. I really do not think he cared and my reaction to the incident pretty much set the tone for the future. I realize now that my lack of reaction set the narrative, right then and there, for how the next ten years would play out.

I did not interrupt his conversation. I waited until it was over to confront him. He instantly turned it on me. It was all my fault. According to him, I was an inadequate wife. Why? Why was it so easy for me to accept the blame for his actions? It was so easy because I did feel inadequate. Who knows how to be what they are not taught either by formal education or influence? Assuming that you can just pick up something new and immediately excel is a poor notion.

Insecure and scared because of all of my past hurts, failed relationships, fears, and rejections, I sought God to save my marriage for the purpose of my image and reputation. I was more in love with the title at this point than I was with the man. I longed to be what they call a good wife. In so many ways, the pain would push me to my purpose. The pain seemed to be my drug of choice as it persisted. I had to go after God.

My husband was always careful to remind me that he never chose to marry a Preacher. Everything was in order. I had asked for and received his permission and before I started down the path to licensure. He seemed to wholeheartedly support me at first. I don't know exactly when the tables turned and at first, I could not understand why. I now think I understand some of the reasons why. Maybe in his mind, by reminding me of this fact, it allowed him the freedom to not be constrained by the standards thereof.

In other words, he was reminding me that since he didn't sign up to be married to a woman of the cloth, he was therefore exempt from living as one. He was reminding me that he was still free. Yet another reason is that people can recognize the spirit within you, and be aggravated by it. I felt unworthy to even have a husband. There had been failed relationships that I had thought would result in marriage but only left wounds- without closure and lack of understanding. With each failure another layer of scar tissue resulted. Since I was not previously good enough to have been a wife to these men of the past, I felt unworthy of my now-husband. The field of inadequacy is fertile ground for seeds of manipulation, control, and abuse to be planted.

• • •

Reflect: Do you feel inadequate? Why? What is causing this feeling? Write it out. Get rid of it.

_____

_____

_____

_____

_____

_____

_____

_____

_____

_____

_____

_____

_____

_____

_____

_____

_____

_____

_____

_____

_____

_____

Points to Ponder:

1. In retrospect, all of the above was too much to be taking into a marriage- any relationship for that matter. I needed counseling and deliverance long before I said "I Do" to both the marriage and the ministry. You really cannot expect wholeness without having healed from brokenness. I had never dealt with any of my baggage. You must first know what a "thing" is, in order to acknowledge it and deal with it. You don't know how to navigate what you can not identify.

2. Before you judge a man or woman of God. Please, remember that we are mere mortals. HUMANS. Not God. Too much faith in any man will only lead to disappointment because without God there is nothing good in a man. We have human emotions, insecurities, faults, and fears. We are messengers.

Finally Free: Totally Bound

I had been delivered from a sinful nature, and I was saved by grace, but I was not free. I was still bound. I did not love myself. I did not care enough about myself to command respect. I didn't even know ME, did not recognize ME. I didn't know my style or have any intimacy with myself. I knew nothing of myself as I had always done what others told me to do or wanted me to do. I lived the life that was mapped out for me by others.

After the first incident of infidelity, I began living this uneasy life, always on pins and needles. I became a wife who was submissive and tolerant of everything, including his repeated lying and cheating. My tolerance for it was seen as acceptance of it, and this became my coping mechanism. I knew what I knew and pretended every day not to know it, just to survive. There were times when the spirit would reveal to me that my (now) ex-husband had been with another woman sexually and I would still roll over on my back and do my wifely duties for him whenever he got back home. I lived in a state of denial that was necessary for survival. After all, what was the alternative?

A few months into the marriage, I was pregnant with our first child together. He was coming home to shower, sleep, and have self-gratifying sex with me. I was obese and miserable and accepted the self-serving sex. Man, man, man.....sex for the married is supposed to be sacred, satisfying, and undefiled. Where the heck was the step-by-step book on how to be a good spouse? How to be a good human? How to please each other selflessly? Has it been written yet? There are so many misconceptions out there and I think at the time, I governed my life by all of them- what a waste. Don't waste your time and or anyone else's. Time can't be recovered.

Reflect: What have you wasted time on that you now resent?

_____

_____

_____

_____

_____

_____

_____

_____

_____

_____

_____

_____

_____

_____

_____

_____

_____

_____

_____

_____

_____

_____

The verbal abuse started during the first year of marriage. I was overweight, as previously stated, and obviously not appealing to my husband. He made it known that thickness was never his forte but that he married me out of sheer love. So, in other words, he was telling me, "I am not attracted to you, but I love you." What the heck does that even mean? I had always been thicker than a snicker- that was all he had ever known me to be. You see where this is going, right? I still wonder what was the true motive for him wanting to marry me. Or, perhaps I did not look bad at all but making me feel insecure was just a method of control.

Then guess what happened? I lost weight. I got a little slim thick. A ray of hope, huh? Perhaps that would make our marriage better??? Perhaps, I could finally gain his undivided attention away from other women. On the contrary, life continually got worse. My ex-husband continued to lie and cheat, just being his genuine self, all the while controlling the narrative at home. He would be gone sometimes for weeks and months at a time and yet still controlled what I did or did not do. I retreated from my family so that they would not know what was going on with me. My thinking was, they wouldn't realize his absence if we all were absent.

I showed up for my shared responsibility of taking care of my grandmother, then went home. I shied away from all family functions. I did not have any prominent friendships outside of family and co-workers. Going to work was so refreshing because it was an outlet from home. But work had to stay at work and could never overlap with home. I could not even mention a co-worker to my husband without being accused of cheating with them.

I struggled to even enjoy church. So much so, that there was really not much reason to attend. Don't get me wrong, I wanted to be there, but my spirit was almost completely depleted by the time that I got out of the house. My attitude and spirit were tormented while I was trying to prepare myself for Gods' facility. Once I arrived at church, I watched the clock constantly during the service. Oftentimes I would have to leave before the benediction if service went too long. This prevented me from being in the posture that I was supposed to be in for God and the Ministry. My Ministry gift was being suppressed.

I caught hell trying to get out of the house to get to church all the way up until the time that I got back home. I could not receive from God what I needed while in His house and He could not use me greatly because I was bound. My ex rarely went to church with me but was somehow still in control. If the church service was longer than normal, I would leave early to keep from having to answer questions from him about what was taking so long. His famous line was, "Church don't last that damn long, who you in there with?" If the altar call at the end of service lasted too long, I was getting back-to-back calls and text messages. Mental and verbal abuse -control, manipulation, mind games- these are all just as detrimental as physical abuse.

I remember so clearly being chastised by a Pastor that was training me. They thought that I was just not doing enough in the church. The whole time they were saying this to me, I thought they had no clue about the hell I would catch when I left the meeting. I also thought to myself, that doing more to be present here, in the church facility itself, might just literally cost me my life. They had no idea what sacrifices I was already making. But God knew.

For thought: Try not to judge people superficially. You never know what a person is going through. Ask the Holy Spirit for discernment. How has judgment impacted relationships with others?

_____

_____

_____

_____

_____

_____

_____

_____

_____

_____

_____

_____

_____

_____

_____

_____

_____

_____

_____

Reflect: Write about a time when you were misjudged:

_____
_____
_____
_____
_____
_____
_____
_____
_____
_____
_____
_____
_____
_____
_____
_____
_____
_____
_____
_____
_____
_____

It seemed like this marriage was going to prevent me from being able to completely walk out my calling but on the contrary in many ways, this marriage was pushing me down the pathway toward the ministry. I knew I was chosen for this walk with God, while at the same time, the enemy was sending a tidal wave down that exact same pathway, trying to drown me before I could get to the other side.

After I lost weight, self-awakening started gradually with the help of God and a good friend. We will call her Angel Coot. She started to implant positive seeds in me daily. She told me I was beautiful in some way or another without effort. **Positive affirmation is contagious**. She prayed with me, she listened to me, she encouraged me, and she included me. The inclusion was therapy; it made me feel worthy of being loved. She never judged me or made me feel ashamed about any part of me. She told me to take care of myself and trust God.

Taking care of myself was something that I had to learn to do again, as I had stopped caring for myself a long time before to just attend to the needs of others. She suggested that I make positive changes to my appearance that helped me feel better about myself. She helped me. She took time out of her day to spend with me. And I will be forever grateful.

• • •

For thought; Take time with your sisters. Someone has to do it. Plant some good seeds. Little things go a long way. Make your sister feel safe and worthy of someone's love and affection. There is so much work for you to do as a woman. Giving others your time generally costs nothing but yields so much. Plan some simple ways you can take time with your sisters.

_____

_____

_____

_____

_____

_____

_____

_____

_____

_____

_____

_____

_____

_____

_____

As I started to come to the knowledge of myself, my husband quickly began to fear that he was losing control, which was true. I was finally beginning to see beyond the limited life he wanted me to live. However, as he became more fearful, the verbal and mental abuse heightened and escalated to physical abuse. Believe me, I know that every couple has their spats. Things are said that aren't meant in the heat of the moment, and sometimes there might be a push or a shove just to create some space. There might even be a light tussle between a couple in highly intense arguments; this is understood. This was not that. The more that I began to awaken and live, the more abrasive the relationship became.

The Breaking Point

I remember the first time that he tried to kill me. It was a calculated and strategic attack of the enemy. I was driving us home from an outing that we had been to with some of my co-workers. Remember, I mentioned before that I could never mix work and home? So, this endeavor was an attempt to connect the two for my spouse and hopefully give him a different outlook to decrease the repeated speculation and accusations. During the outing, he started accusing me of being in a relationship with one of my co-workers. We actually left the gathering early because I could sense that he was "fin to show out," and I did not want him to make a scene in front of my co-workers.

On the way home, he tried to instigate an argument with me over this co-worker. My unwillingness to argue back heightened his rage, and it was as if he was transformed. As I was driving down the highway home, he took over the steering wheel from the passenger side and steered us off the road into the grassy area of an off-ramp. I had to have been going at least 60 miles per hour while driving an SUV. By the grace of God, we were not traveling in the passing lane, and there was no other lane between us and the greenery. It's a miracle in itself that he didn't flip the car and kill us both. I hit the brakes and the car came to a stop. He pulled me out of the car from my seat, through the passenger side door, and onto the ground, where he beat the hell out of me. To this day, I don't even remember how the car gear got into 'Park' because it all happened so quickly. I just remember him on top of me, just pounding and pounding and pounding...

Some people from another car stopped and started recording on their phones while asking me if I wanted them to call the police. I was screaming for them to help me, but they just kept recording. They never came over to help me, and the police never arrived. I am not sure what made him stop, but he suddenly got off of me. He took my cell phone from the car and threw it out into the grass where I could not find it to call for help, and he left on foot. The keys were still in the car with the ignition running. I got in the car and drove home. When I got there, I nursed my wounds. I threw away the shirt that was torn almost off of me. I had borrowed a leather jacket for that nights' event from Angel Coot. I washed it thoroughly. Thankfully, it was not damaged. That next working day, I had it ready to return to her. I never ever told her what that jacket had been through. I never called the police and never told my family (they are reading about this at the same time that you are).

For Thought: It is important to note here that the physical abuse started exactly one year before I started my Ministry In Training program. You have to be able to see the enemy and his strategies. The thing that one would least suspect. 2 Corinthians 2:11 warns Lest Satan should get an advantage of us: for we are not ignorant of his devices. What connections like this have you seen in your life?

_____

_____

_____

_____

_____

_____

_____

_____

_____

_____

_____

_____

_____

_____

I was not mature enough to completely understand the strategic attack, but I surely do now. The car accidents from earlier in my life had not taken me out, so now the enemy decided to change his tactics in order to try to counteract those precise failed attempts. He was going to use the thing closest to me to kill me. He had to keep my mouth closed at all costs. Killing me would have aborted God's ultimate plan for my life. Writing of this incident does not glorify the devil but proves Luke 10:19, "I have given you authority to trample on snakes and scorpions and to overcome all the power of the enemy; nothing will harm you," and Philippians 1:6, "Being confident of this, that he who began a good work in you will carry it on to completion until the day of Christ Jesus."

For Thought: When the enemy goes to such lengths to kill you, you must be carrying something dangerous. You are a threat. Ask the Lord to show you what you are carrying that is so dangerous and threatening to the enemy that he wants to take you out. You are dangerous and needed for Kingdom warfare.

_____

_____

_____

_____

_____

_____

_____

_____

_____

_____

_____

_____

_____

_____

_____

_____

He returned home a couple of days later and acted as if nothing had happened, and I went along with it. I really cannot blame anyone else for what I allowed but myself. Sometimes I have found myself so angry. Angry at God, wondering how this could be allowed or condoned by Him if I was indeed his chosen vessel. Why would he allow me to be treated with such cruelty, pain, and sheer humiliation? Now, I understand the simple principle of reaping and sowing. I have not been an angel, nor do I profess to be one. I have sown many bad seeds. So, I do understand that I was due something back because of the negative seeds I had sown. I indeed did reap. But man, oh man, there was no way that I deserved all that I went through.

I will not torment myself by recounting all of the instances of abuse, misuse, and neglect--even while pregnant with his children. We will keep on moving. Just remember to pray for wisdom so that you will not be ignorant. Ask for discernment and spiritual intuition specifically for sight to see the hand of the enemy; He does indeed intend to attempt to sift you as wheat every chance that he gets. Stay covered and connected. You will need an "Angel Coot" in your corner. Pray and specifically ask God for your earthly Angel to present themselves if you are at a place where you cannot readily identify them.

I need to state here that I am not condoning or excusing physical abuse in any way. I am not justifying or excusing any form of abuse, for that matter, because it all creates lasting, sometimes irreversible, scars. I am simply stating my truths. Do not make the same decision to stay silent that I did. If you are in an abusive relationship. Get some help. Reach out to a friend, your minister, a counselor, a stranger, anyone. God will provide a source that you can trust if you ask him to. Just know there is the possibility of life on the other side. You must not allow fear of the unknown to hold you in bondage.

Preach Anyway

One of the first sermons that I prepared and preached was entitled the *Power of Pain*, based on James 1:2. The request to preach on this particular occasion was impromptu. I did not have time to prepare in the natural realm. The Holy Spirit had to give the vision for the message and the anointing to deliver it.

I was sho'nuff preaching to myself. It was almost like a foreshadowing of life to come. It took me to this day, at this very moment, to understand that I was speaking prophetically over my own life. I remember searching the bible for a word to preach, and the scripture seemed to jump off the page. I struggled with this Word because I knew it was not going to be what people wanted to hear. No one wants to be told that pain can be purposeful. I struggled with how I would make it make sense. The struggle was so unfruitful and unnecessary. In the end, I trusted God, went forth, and He spoke through me. This remains one of the most profound sermons that I have ever rendered because it first ministered to me.

Take a moment and place yourself in a pulpit of a fairly large Baptist church, where you stand before about 400 or 500 people to declare the goodness of God to the masses with full confidence, passion, and under the anointing of God. After you preach and fill the lives of others with the living word of God, it's back to reality. There is absolutely nothing standing between you and the abusive relationship waiting for you at home after the close of the service.

For me, home equaled Hell on Earth. I would drive home in silence, praying that God had shown up and showed out at my house. I was wondering if God had regulated things while I was doing his work at the church. After all, I had just finished decreeing that better days were coming, so those things just had to manifest at my house, right? I remember just sitting in the driveway, dreading going inside. I wanted to give it all up because I could not tangibly see God moving. He was not working how I wanted Him to work; He was not moving how I would have preferred that He move.

As I told you before, death was invited and welcomed. I felt like I was out of options. At the time, death, for me, would have been the ultimate win. My children would have been taken care of financially and I would have peace. The devil would no longer be able to torment me. I was never suicidal, but always willing to die. Why not suicide? I fought too hard in hell on earth to die and go to hell.

But God never allowed the devil to take my life. And what's even crazier is that every time, with every attack, every choke, every threat, I woke up more and more. I became more aware. Instead of becoming more and more lifeless, I was becoming more and more purposeful.

God was ultimately working on my behalf the whole time I was attending to his assignments. He was covering me, protecting me, preserving me, and perfecting my purpose, unbeknownst to me. My spiritual vision and purpose became more and more clear with every assault whether verbal or physical. **For every wound, there was an awakening. I am sure the enemy thought he was killing me in the natural because I was being crushed on every side. In actuality, this was all growing my spirit man. The wounds were adding water to the seed planted in fertile ground.**

As time went on, I became more and more confident in myself as I kept preaching confidence in God. "Consequently, faith comes from hearing the message, and the message is heard through the word about Christ" (Romans 10:17). I got so good with God that I could actually go to bed and lay down next to the enemy, snore, and fear not. I knew God was not going to let me perish--not by my own asking nor by the enemy taking. **Preaching and teaching through pain perfected my purpose and gifted me with anointing and power.**

● ● ●

For thought: If you do not get anything else from reading this section of the book. I want you to leave with this: Let NO THING and NO ONE cancel the work of the Lord assigned to your person. His WILL has to be done. It doesn't matter who or what situations come, you will not die until your purpose on the earth has been fulfilled, even if you want to die. God's word concerning you will not return to Him void. You will not return to your Heavenly Father until your work has been done. So, Get After It! Gone and preach! Preach to yourself if no one else will listen.

_____

_____

_____

_____

_____

_____

_____

_____

_____

_____

_____

Damage is not damnation, brokenness can be beautiful, wounds make warriors, attacks incite anointing, and pain produces power.

Reflect: We all have pain points, things that have happened in your life that bring you pain or fear. Write about your pain points. Allow your feelings to flow, it can be therapeutic.

_____

_____

_____

_____

_____

_____

_____

_____

_____

_____

_____

_____

_____

_____

_____

Why I Stayed

I need to talk through my truths as to why I stayed. This is always the question that people most want to know the answer to. I am going to answer as best I can based upon my rationale at that particular time, no matter how obscured it may seem today. Never say what you will or will not do. Never say what you will not tolerate because you don't know what you will or won't do until faced with the situation. It is so easy to judge a situation and make a declaration about how you would govern yourself in that space before it becomes your individual reality.

Simply put, I did not want to be single again. I did not want to be a single parent again. There was so much fear of the unknown. Life as I knew it was hell but at least it was familiar. Over time, I grew to know the demons that I would face daily, very well. I had become comfortable with managing them. It was easier, I thought at the time, to face the demons that were familiar to me than to take a chance at the unknown. I had already raised two children without their father in the home and did not want to put this stigma onto any more of my children. I had been the daughter of an absent father. I knew firsthand what it was like to long for unconditional love from your father and not be able to get it because you could not find them.

As my children's protector, sacrificing myself was nothing to help ensure their security. I believed a male figure in the home was better than none at all. The logic that escaped me at that time was, what was I teaching my children by staying in an unhealthy relationship? I did not consider what they were learning to accept and tolerate based upon their observations of me. I was not teaching my sons how to treat women by my example, and I was not teaching my daughters what to expect from a husband. These are the makings of generational curses. Me choosing to stay to avoid the unfamiliar was doing my children a terrible disservice. I truly thought that I was protecting them by continuing to live this way, but in reality, I was placing us all in a pit that we all would have to eventually have to deal with and be freed from.

For a woman of the cloth, being married feels like a must. It is hard enough for a woman to be accepted as a minister of God, let alone a single one. Even in the 21st Century, there are still many that do not believe in women preaching or Pastoring. My own father held this belief. He refused to support me as a preacher. He refused to come and hear me preach my first message. I remember the day I called to invite him. He simply said, "I won't be there. I don't believe in women preachers but thank you for calling." I remember being in a state of shock, but I was not hurt. I did not feel any pain. I was numb in that space and accustomed to him not showing up for any life event concerning me.

There had really only ever been a couple of consistent male figures in my life that poured anything into my well-being, and they were my maternal uncles. My father was rejecting me and the God in me. Oh ok!!!..."What then shall we say in response to these things? If God is for us, who can be against us" (Romans 8:31).

I went forward anyway. In my mind, there were countless times when I had disappointed God and I determined that ministry and marriage were two spaces where I wanted to keep my vows, no matter what. These instances above are things that I wanted to spare my kids from, therefore taking whatever measures I could to hold the family together, giving them a father of some kind in the home.

Having been raised in and practicing ministry in a traditional Baptist church, my title was important. I was concerned about the so-called "order of things." There are so many titles that I wanted to add to my signature line and above all, it seemed that being "Mrs." was the most important one to attain and sustain. It was important to stay within my marriage for the sake of the image of my ministry. **Fear and insecurity sometimes were more prevalent than faith in my life in those days.** The society of the "church" is difficult to navigate. Church can easily become more about pleasing people than pleasing God if you are not careful. Religion and tradition will consume you and can completely make you miss your relationship with Christ if you are not cautious. This was me at that time. **The façade of religion had fully replaced actual**

faith-based belief. I began to be able to comprehend why so many believers had fallen away from the faith. I now understood things that I had once incorrectly judged.

Reflect: Where and when have you felt rejected or fearful? How did you deal with this rejection and/or fear? How did you resolve the situation?

_____

_____

_____

_____

_____

_____

_____

_____

_____

_____

_____

_____

_____

_____

_____

_____

_____

_____

_____

For thought: Without a true relationship with God, there is no revelation. Without revelation, there is no declaration of purpose, and without a purpose, there is nothing to press towards. What is your purpose?

_____

_____

_____

_____

_____

_____

_____

_____

_____

_____

_____

_____

_____

_____

_____

_____

_____

_____

_____

_____

Of course, as indicated, I realize today that my logic was so far off and misguided but this was my truth at that moment. These reasons were the basis of why I stayed. I do not ask for understanding of the reasons, just acceptance that this is my truth. I believe if we would all be honest with ourselves; we would have a greater capacity for understanding the situations where fictitious logic governed our decision-making. Maturing changes our narrative over time. Your awakening will happen; trust God. It really will happen. I am a witness.

• • •

Fruit of the Spirit

"For God's gifts and his call are irrevocable" (Romans 11:29).

Spiritual gifts started to manifest again about fifteen years ago before I was married. I emphasize the word "again" because I have memories of having encounters with the Holy Spirit as a child when I would attend church with my great-grandmother. The spirit would be so high in that old wooden-floored church, that as the church mothers would sing the old hymns, I could actually see angels in action. I could see them, right there in our midst. Of course, I did not understand and never spoke to my Big Momma about my experiences because I did not think that she would believe me. I now know that what I saw was real and that I was, in fact, entertaining angels. God was pouring out his spirit upon me even then by allowing me a glimpse into another dimension.

"In the last days, God says, I will pour out my Spirit on all people. Your sons and daughters will prophesy, your young men will see visions, your old men will dream dreams" (Acts 2:17).

I knew before marriage that my husband was coming because I saw it in a vision. God gave me the order of things, how it was to progress. I had written down all that I saw in the vision. So, when my now ex-husband presented himself and asked me to marry him, I did not ponder long over what to do. Oh yes, I know what you are thinking but bear with me, it's going to come together.

We had known each other for seven months before getting married. It does not take a smart person to realize that he did not 'know me-know me' and I did not 'know him-know him.' All that escaped me at the time, however, because I knew what I heard God say would happen, and more than that, I knew what I wanted to happen. My biological clock was ticking, and it was time that I get married. I felt like I had the green light from God, and it was ok to move forward. I did not ask for confirmation because I knew what I had seen and heard. We attended a round of premarital counseling, and that was that. I think during the counseling sessions we presented the couple that the counselors needed to see in order to get approval.

I now acknowledge that I ignored all of the warning signs around me. I overlooked the warning signs and red flags because I wanted to be married and believed, without a shadow of a doubt, that I had God's blessing. He was a man living life for himself and himself only. Still to this day, fourteen years later, he still does not know me, even after eleven years of marriage.

As I have said previously, the misfires of the marriage pushed into complete surrender to God. The darker life got, the more in touch with God I became. **I dialed deep into Him. Not only to hear but to listen.** Yes, there is a difference. I will also say this, and I have to say this! I know that I hear from God, and I know beyond a shadow of a doubt that God lives in me. There have been too many times that I have heard him speak to me, then I have turned around and spoken what he has given me to whomever it applied to and seen it manifest. There have been too many accounts and too many witnesses to discredit my gifting in this area. I have, however, still questioned God because of all that I am sharing with you that I went through. I felt like I missed what He was trying to tell me concerning marriage. Particularly as it relates to my ex-husband. To date, God has only given me two words concerning the matter: counterfeit and necessary.

Everything that I went through was necessary. Know this, once God gives you a vision and/or a dream, protect and guard it at all costs. You cannot trust visions and dreams to those that do not share your same spiritual placement. They won't get it and won't help you labor for it.. If you are not careful, they might even talk you into aborting it! Beyond that, if you don't fully understand what you are seeing or hearing, go to the elders that you trust and get some guidance. Visions and dreams can be for immediate manifestation or for the future.

For example, think about how long of a time span there was in between the prophecy of Jesus' birth and the time that it actually came to fruition. The enemy can see, and he can hear.

He is waiting for the right opportunity to interrupt what God has working in your life. He is the author of confusion. Just like we as black people take pride in our appearance and putting our best foot forward, the enemy knows how to present himself in his 'Sunday best' as well. Enough said about that.

For thought: Study your gifts as you are given them. Study them to know exactly what they are, when to use them, how to protect them and how to work through them. This is very important. Your gifting matures as your relationship with Him deepens. Some visions and dreams are for immediate manifestation, some are preparation for the future. What have you been gifted with?

_____

_____

_____

_____

_____

_____

_____

_____

_____

_____

_____

_____

_____

_____

_____

I used to say right is right and wrong is wrong, period, until today. Now, I realize that I was wrong to think about it in such simplicity. It's not that simple. Right versus wrong is not just black and white. There are shades of grey.

This is my rationale for making this statement. Because everyone does not have the same morals, standards, and foundational principles. Therefore everyone's perception of what is right and wrong can be very, very different. This is why people cannot agree on seemingly simple concepts. This was a major learning for me. You cannot, no matter how hard you try, convince a person that does not share your same foundational principles of anything whether right or wrong. It's a lost cause and a complete waste of time.

When looking for a mate, look at their core. I have a whole other appreciation for 2 Corinthians 6:14 and the importance of being equally yoked. Its faith, core values, and belief systems, too. I believe it's the core beliefs that are what is going to keep you together or keep you distant. One cannot have any understanding in an unfamiliar place. They do not have the capacity. Better to realize that they don't have the capacity early on than to waste your energy being confused. You will forever be upset trying to figure out why they do not get it or get you.

• • •

For example, I was told that I should not be afraid of my ex-husband because I am physically strong. I was totally confused and bewildered by the statement. Whether or not I have the physical capacity to hold my own, why should I have to? What happened to the basic principle that a woman should not have to be put in a place that she should have to defend herself against a man? What happened to a husband being a protector and not a predator? The bible says a man is to love his wife as Christ loved the church. Christ gave his life for the church. Walk away in harmony when you recognize that these core values do not match. You do not deserve to live in chaos.

People will try to discredit your experience if acceptance of it makes them uncomfortable. Just because a person does not believe and/or validate your experience does not mean that it's false. **Embrace your truth, learn from it, and lead with it.** I have learned that people have different types of coping mechanisms. Sometimes it's easier for a person to discredit and dismiss you than to face the fact that there might be a defect in their camp.

ISLAND (In His Safety, Love and Newness Develop)

There is this thing that I like to call the ISLAND phase. As you awaken, there is this strange feeling that comes over you. The best analogy that I can make is to compare that feeling to that of being either on an island or being the island itself. Don't shy away from it. Embrace it as a necessary part of your process.

An island can be described as a piece of land surrounded by water and/or a body of land that is isolated and detached in some way. You may feel like you are an island, totally isolated from everyone and all alone. You feel surrounded on every side by obstacles that seem insurmountable. Even if you're physically surrounded by people you can still feel quite alone. This feeling of being isolated, surrounded but yet alone, is a crazy, crazy feeling that causes a great deal of fear and animosity. Doubt is one of the things that circles about you. You wonder if you are making a mistake in finally starting to care about yourself.

If you are one that has a people-pleasing personality, you may even find yourself feeling guilty because now you have to change your narrative. Your focus has to move from them to you now which makes you feel a little out of balance at first. As it should, right? This is an unfamiliar place.

● ● ●

I am here to encourage you not to back away from your ISLAND experience. I promise you, even though you feel isolated, this is a necessary step. In isolation, your consecration process is at work within you. You are not alone. You are right where the Father needs you to be so that he can have your undivided attention. Throw your hands up, tilt your head back, and let God know you are here for whatever he needs to work out in your ISLAND phase.

* * *

Released

The last two incidents of physical abuse involved two of my four children who were quite young; my infant daughter and adolescent son. On one occasion, I remember being pushed down into the corner between the front door and the closet door. My ex-husband was standing over me with his fist drawn back, ready to strike. As I looked up at him, I just remember hearing my son screaming, "Get off my momma!" at the top of his lungs. My son began to swing in my defense with a type of supernatural power and strength. It scared me.

Afterward, I immediately started to look at my life in an entirely different way. I had already pretty much given up on my own life and pursuit of my own happiness. Now I began to think about my son and what he was learning as a result of what he witnessed at home. If he repeated this behavior as he saw it, it would be my fault. As a child, he should not have been in a place to have to act as my protector. The roles were out of order. I also began to wonder if my daughter knew what was actually happening in her little head and how this may be affecting her development.

On that particular occasion, my neighbor heard the altercation, overhearing my son's screaming, and called the police. By the time the police came to the door, my ex had already left the house. I told my son not to say a word, and he complied. I told the police that the neighbor was mistaken. They asked if they could see the children in person as well as examine me. They looked us over, we were all physically fine - there were no visible injuries. As I talked to the officer, however, my back was in so much pain that I felt like I was going to fall forward into his chest. I stood as straight as I could until he left, holding my baby in my dominant hand. After the officers left, I could not even really allow myself to focus on my physical pain. I needed to attend to the needs of my son. God had blessed me with this child and trusted me to care for him in all ways. This could not possibly be healthy for him. I was too embarrassed and ashamed to change for me, but I was now fully unwilling to sacrifice the well-being of my babies. Motherhood would win over self. I knew separation and divorce were inevitable at this point.

Feeling like divorce disqualified me from service to God, the first thing I did was retreat. I retreated and withdrew from all of my ministry assignments - both public and private. In a way, I even retreated from God. I stopped reading, studying, writing, and praying. I did not understand why God would allow this to happen to his servant. I was very angry with God, to say the least.

I felt like I had trusted God with everything, exchanged my will for His will, and I just had absolutely no understanding as to how He could allow this to be. I felt forsaken. I began to question everything. I even started to see why it was so easy for people to believe that there was no God. I planned to never preach or teach again. After all, you cannot preach and teach to someone else unless that word first ministers to you. I could not encourage myself, much less anyone else. I was beyond furious, angry, and defensive every minute of every day. I felt entitled to be angry.

For as angry and rebellious as I was at the time, God still kept calling my name. I kept having the notion of operating in my spiritual gifts even though I felt lost. People still needed me and still looked to me for encouragement. God kept speaking to me, and the visions and dreams He sent, were increasing in frequency and urgency, despite my wrong and unwilling attitude. How could God see, hear, and yet still allow these things to happen to me?

I wanted to know what I had done wrong to deserve all of this hell. Don't get me wrong. As I said before, I knew that I had to reap those bad seeds that I had previously sown, but even taking into account all I had done wrong in my life, it simply did not seem to add up to all of these years of suffering. Where was the balance?

The last physical assault was a blow to the head. It was the most painful, the most threatening to my life, and also most impactful and life-changing. Just like the woman at the well, she had to go to draw water at the particular time that she did in order to get what she needed from Jesus. There was no other way it could happen for her.

Just like Jesus had to die for our salvation, it had to happen that way. I am not condoning violence or giving anyone justification to hurt someone else. What I am saying here, is that the weapon formed will not prosper but it will be used. **Let your pain be the footstool that elevates you up and over to your next level.**

I remember being hit so hard that I could not hear out of my left ear. I vividly remember the feeling of my brain shifting within my skull. But guess what, I stayed on my feet. I remained standing and looked the enemy right in the face. I was holding my baby and still did not lose my grip on her. I did not faint or fall. At that moment, my life completely changed. It was like I was fortified. In the natural, I felt a shift within my skull, while in the spiritual realm there was also a shift. God said, "That's enough you are released. Your work in this space, this level, is done. You can go." God liberated me and freed me to move forward with clear Godly consciousness.

Reflect: What do you need to be freed from?

_____

_____

_____

_____

_____

_____

_____

_____

_____

_____

_____

_____

_____

_____

_____

_____

_____

_____

_____

_____

_____

_____

_____

Ministry after Divorce

What happened after the separation and subsequent divorce was nothing like I expected. This is why the Bible says, His ways are not our ways and His thoughts are not our thoughts (see Isaiah 55:8-9). I expected to be cast away from the ministry so, in anticipation, I retreated. I was prepared to give up "The Call" just to be free. I took the initiative to cast myself out, saving anyone else from having to do it. Despite this, I learned that God would still find me. Please understand that there is no freedom outside of the Will of God.

He kept calling my name, He kept speaking to me, He kept sending people my way for me to encourage and pray for me. He kept sending visions and dreams. He kept being in my business, where I did not want Him at the moment. The farther I ran and harder I tried to hide, the harder it became to escape God. I was boxed in, no outlet. It does not matter how high you are, how low, what you try to do, or what you refuse to do. You cannot get past God. Whom He has called He has also predestined (see Romans 8:30). He was patient with me, He was long-suffering.

The opportunities to preach and teach kept coming. I preached this time from a different place. **Out of pain, purpose was birthed and power was manifested. Out of my discomfort developed a ministry of deliverance**. I began to have to speak and teach out of my brokenness. There was more power in my delivery. There was a greater authority in my declaration.

I know now that truly, God was God. Not only because I read, studied, and heard others tell of his goodness, but because I have personally witnessed Him be Almighty in my presence. I would never have made it any other way. I know that sounds cliché, but it is the truth. God wouldn't let me die. He had a hedge of protection placed around my life. I began to be put in spaces where it was absolutely necessary to share bits of my personal story as I spoke on the goodness of Jesus. His healing and resurrecting power was evident in my being alive. My experiences created an impact and confirmed every word of God to be true. Not only did I live through, but I came into a new anointing and a new level on the other side of my pain.

Divine Connections

Nothing missing, nothing broken. It's easy for us as believers to trust God to be a provider when we are talking about material things and possessions. This mentality, however, actually limits the capacity of God. God is able to do ALL things. He is a provider of everything we need, even those things that we don't even know we need. Omnipotent God has given provisions even before there is a manifested need. For this reason, there is no need to force relationships of any kind. The bible says in Matthew 6:33, "But seek first His kingdom and His righteousness, and all these things will be given to you as well." This promise stretches so far as to even include personal relationships. Do not force relationships with people, whether friends or blood relatives.

If you trust Him, God will ordain and appoint each person that is assigned to your life and vice versa. God will move the Heavens to provide for you. Even if He has to physically move you into a new space, perhaps a new job, a new city, or a new relationship, just to cause you to connect with your destiny, He will. Trust God completely. Truly his ways are not our ways and thoughts not our thoughts. Our thoughts cannot conceive the methodology of Christ.

During my season of separation and divorce, times were really hard for me all the way around. Not only financially but mentally. I needed a lot and was broken in so many places. People that I expected to be there for me during those times were nowhere to be found. Most weren't available and some just did not want to be bothered. At first, this angered me because I expected people to be there for me as I had been for them. Again, I was too busy playing the victim and not counting the victories in my life. The removal of layers was an intentional act of God. When I totally let go and just moved with the waves God made, then things began to come together. God supernaturally orchestrated a new network tailor-made just for me. I thought God moved me to a specific location in life to provide one thing, but in all reality, it was a setup for Him to be glorified in another way.

Looking at things with the natural eye, we may never actually get to see them for what they truly are. God gave me an ordained circle of friends. All of us are so very different, however, the difference makes a masterpiece. It's like a patchwork quilt. It starts with fragments, but when it's all put together, it's beautiful, you can no longer see where one piece starts or stops. I have my own circle of earthly angels. We are called to support each other and to help each other into our own destiny, even if it means painfully pushing one another out of a comfort zone.

Everything that God does, He does well. Though the storms come and go, my circle is strong and unbreakable because it's God-composed. Trust God. I tell you He cares for every place, every portion of your being. Be not concerned with who you may have lost or shed along the way. God has it worked out and fully mapped out. Keep moving and keep looking ahead. He will never leave you lacking in anything, no matter how great or small it seems. What God ordains will last 4ever4life.

Faith Forward

So here we are, at the end of a chapter, the closing of my section. The blessing is that this ending births a new beginning. In the paragraphs above, I have told my story, The PREACHER {Peace Reached Even After Complete Hell (with) Everything Restored} the anointed Woman of God, who became a willing vessel of the Lord, years into a tumultuous marriage. A marriage that started out, out of order and was tainted from the start. I've shown what happens when an unevenly yoked union collides with a spiritual calling. I have discussed a separation, the reservations around leaving, and the ultimate end of a marriage.

What I hope that I have demonstrated to you through my life's experience is that God is God. He can choose to set apart and use whomever he wants to, even the lowly of us. Once God consecrates you for his purpose, it does not matter who or what comes against you; you can not and will not be defeated. You cannot lose. You might lose a few battles along the way, but you will not lose the war. Everything, every weapon, and every obstacle God will use for good and for his glorification.

Now we arrive at a place where I am no longer going to speak in the past tense. It is time for me to demonstrate to you what exercising extreme faith actually looks like. This is the place where I have to write what I expect to see before it manifests itself. God has impressed it upon me to go ahead and write this vision, making it plain. Now, on this day in May of 2020, I have to write this according to what I saw in the spirit realm and trust God to bring all this to pass in the natural realm in the time that he has set. Let me start with ministry. Isaiah 60:22 says, "The least of you will become a thousand, the smallest a mighty nation. I am the Lord; in its time I will do this swiftly."

In the years to come, my ministry will be a ministry of deliverance. I will preach and teach the gospel and help usher those who desire it, straight to deliverance. Deliverance will come through the confessed need to change and the acknowledgment that we cannot do it on our own. The testimony of myself and others will serve as witnesses to the unchanging love and the consistency of Almighty God.

I am living proof of God's grace, mercy, and immeasurable resurrecting power. As I usher in deliverance God will continue to perfect my spiritual gifts and allow me to flow therein as needed. The gifts of tongues, wisdom, miracles, healing and prophecy, as needed for the advancement of the Kingdom and as led by the Holy Spirit for the glorification of God. He has, through all of my pain, imparted everything that I need to sustain myself and others. I asked God clearly what is my position in your workforce? **He replied to me, "You are a**

vessel of supernatural breakthrough for yourself and others in the Kingdom." I am now in complete surrender and total compliance with what is asked of me!

On paper, I am not worthy of being used by God for anything! I am humbled that He would still even choose to use me. At this point, I've had a few months off from work, and at home, it's been just Jesus and me. God has been different with me in this quiet time at home, or shall I say, I have been different with Him. God has always been there; it's me that was wavering and not always attentive to His need for my life because of my own struggles. I understand that I was not available nor open to being God's mouthpiece at times where it was inconvenient for me. **He revealed to me that I had been too busy being the victim instead of counting the victories.** Even though I was going through turmoil, He was still fighting for me. And He was winning.

Ownership

Over time, I have learned that an important part of healing is taking ownership of what you allow. There is a lot that I allowed to happen to me because of my own instability. I do not want it to be perceived that I am playing the victim card because there could be no victimizer without a victim. In my case, I have to acknowledge here that a very good friend helped me to realize that acknowledgement really is not all that is required to move forward; you must also take responsibility for the part that you played.

Now I believe that God is ok with trusting me to go to the next realm of the spirit. He has been preparing me, and this time of solitude has allowed him to do what he wanted with me. My ministry will be BIG for his glory, and I will willingly GO without boundaries or limitations.

• • •

My New and Forever Husband is on the Horizon

Oh my God! He will manifest himself soon and very soon. I am in a position for him to come and retrieve me. I am working the fields and minding God's business. **I am not in pursuit of a man; I am in pursuit of God.** He has promised to give me the desires of my heart if I delight myself in Him. The marriage will be in order, with God as the head, my husband next, and I will follow. He will love me with the same love that God has for the church. He will come in and restore all that the locusts and cankerworms have taken from me (see Joel 1:4). He will support me and encourage me in what is necessary for my life, family, ministry, and marriage. He will be my provider, my security, my sanity, and my peace on earth.

The love that we will share will be beyond the physical and could only be orchestrated by God. He will be my best friend and confidant for real. He will be a King and a Warrior. He will keep me covered in all my endeavors. There will be nothing missing and nothing broken. As God has healed me in the spirit realm, my husband will heal me in the natural. Healing will be found in his heart, arms, and hands. My brokenness will be beautiful to him, and he will love every part of me, even the crazies.

• • •

I will be his helpmeet, his peace, his portion of favor with God, his prayer warrior, and his number one fan. We will be each other's "good thing," and together we will change the world. The blending of our families will come easily as all things of the Lord do. Nothing for me to do but wait. God will reveal all to him and I will respond in order.

Yep, I'm still the PREACHER, with a resounding newness of anointing, grace, and purpose. I survived. What the enemy sought out to use to destroy me, has perfected me and given me my true purpose. God preserved me through it all for His glory.

"I consider that our present sufferings are not worth comparing with the glory that will be revealed in us" (Romans 8:18).

The blessings of the Lord are ye and amen. No good thing will He withhold from his children, (see Psalm 84:11). Finally, ALL things work together for the good (see Romans 8:28). These things I have written as they ARE even though they BE NOT, and as the Holy Spirit gave me utterance.

For whoever has read this portion, my final words to you are...**God Will!**

Maybe you cannot, but God can, and He will! God will do what needs to be done to ensure that your purpose is fulfilled in the earth, for His glorification. No matter what your current state is, God has the final say. The path may not be straight, but you are going to get to where you have to go. You will arrive at your destination on time. Trust God. God will.

Selah

Acknowledgments

To God, my savior, redeemer, keeper, and provider...(just to name a few things.) Thank you for choosing me when I didn't know to choose you.

To my father, the late Lawrence Massey Jr., and my mother Carolyn Straite, thank you for giving me life and a chance in this world.

Kenton, Kara, Chaise and Doriann, and my granddaughter Chamberlain, thanks for giving me a reason to persevere.

To my siblings, April, Carmesia, Decario, and Trina I am blessed and honored to be your big sister.

To the brothers Stewart McDay and Ray Bennett, you have adopted me as your little sister and have never let me down.

To my Godmother, Gwendolyn Jones, one of my first images of a phenomenal woman was found in you.

To my 4ever4life sisters, thank you for accepting me. Thank you for trusting me enough to participate in this God-given vision.

● ● ●

Diesel, thank you for helping the damaged me to heal. Thanks for showing me what unconditional love looks like. Thanks for pushing me and encouraging me to be better and to go after it all.

My prayer warriors, Taleitha Williams, Cassandra Dervin, Evangelist Maggie Gettys, and Karen Sanders....you held me up!

To all of my family and friends. Love you and thank God for each of you.

I salute Eric Straite, The GOAT.

In memory of: Lawrence Massey, Sr., Barbara J. Massey, Leverne Massey, Edward, and Gertrude Davis. Moses Straite, Jr., Hazeline Straite, and James E. Straite, Hazel Mackey and Margaret Mackey and Fred Rowe

I salute the late Sadie M. Rowe and Dorothy A Lee who were both instrumental in teaching me how to be a woman and who filled every void that they possibly could throughout my life.

Yours in Service,
Tijuana

Closing

In closing, we; The Professional, The Celebrity, The Unicorn, and The Preacher, pray that some portion of this book has caused you to become a better you. Perhaps you were able to relate to one of the storylines presented, perhaps you will share one of the testimonies you read, perhaps God gave you revelation while reading. Whatever you have received, just know that it was God ordained.

You are worthy and you are more than enough.

It's a common practice for us to look to God and trust Him with relationships when we are talking about male/female relationships-dating and marriage. We challenge you to let God lead you into ordained friendships as well. We are witnesses that he will lead you into a circle of connections that will have stronger bonds than blood.

We are a group of women who are so profoundly different in all areas. Our ages range from 31 to 50. We are all from different cities of origin and have different family makeups. We all have different likes and dislikes with variations of degrees and life goals. We have different struggles and strengths. We are all broken but together function as an unstoppable force. Our cohesiveness was easy and unlabored.

● ● ●

God used a place as a connector for us. That place was just the foundation for things we could not foresee or imagine.

All we know is that God did it. He placed us together, and there is no other connection like ours that we have ever experienced. Everything that He does, He does it well. God is peculiar and specializes in things that do not make sense. It was not by our choosing but by God's ordination that we became an unbreakable unit.

We are sisters, 4ever4life. Our Weird works.

Made in the USA
Columbia, SC
22 July 2021

42238749R00137